Dr.

WRESTLING WITH GOD

How Can I Love a God I'm Not Sure I Trust?

Printed in Canada through Givington's.

Dr. Jim Denison

WRESTLING WITH GOD

How Can I Love a God I'm Not Sure I Trust?

Table of Contents

Preface V
Acknowledgments IX
Introduction: Wondering About God XI

Part 1: Why Wrestle with God?

Chapter 1: Why Believe a Two-Thousand-Year-Old Book? 1
Chapter 2: If God Is Real, Why Aren't We Sure? 19
Chapter 3: If Christianity Is True, Why Aren't Christians Better People? 35
Chapter 4: Is Jesus Really God? 53
Chapter 5: Is Jesus the Only Way to God? 71

Part 2: The Hardest Questions Christians Ask

Chapter 6: Where Was God When My Father Died? 95
Chapter 7: When Suffering Makes No Sense 111
Chapter 8: Did God Cause My Father's Death? 131
Chapter 9: What Happens to Those Who Never Hear? 153
Chapter 10: Does Prayer Really Work? 189
Chapter 11: Why Doesn't God Always Give Us What We Ask For? 205

Conclusion: A Man with Two Names 223
Appendix 225
Recommended Reading 241
Endnotes 249

DEDICATION

To Janet
The love of my life and joy of my heart

To our sons and their families
God's best gifts

To friends in four churches
Being your pastor has been my great honor

To the memory of Lester I. Denison
Finally, I understand

PREFACE

Most days, I have all of God I want. My life is good: My family is blessed, God is blessing our ministry, my work seems successful. But I know that God wants a more intimate relationship with me than he and I have today. He wants me to love him with unbridled passion and trust him without reservation. I'll be honest—I don't, at least not often enough.

Part of the problem is that my life is too hectic and scheduled, without enough time for solitude and communion with God. But even my busyness is a reaction to the real problem. I have questions about God, issues that keep me from wanting to trust him more than I do.

It's hard to depend on someone who has disappointed you. (It's only natural to pull back, to minimize your risk and cut your losses, to decide not to let the person who hurt you hurt you again.) You may still have a relationship with that person. You may stay married, or keep your job, or maintain your friendship. But you won't expose yourself to further pain. More often than not, a liar will lie again. A thief will likely steal again. At the very least, you want the person to prove that things have changed before you'll believe they have.

So it is with my relationship with God. It's easy to confuse *working for* God with *walking with* God. Many of us who are religious professionals make this well-intentioned mistake. But that's not my real problem. The real reason why my life is so hectic is so I'll have a convenient excuse for not being closer to God. I'm so busy serving him that I don't have time to know him better. But it's not because I love him so much—it's because I don't. I don't really want to spend more time with him in prayer and worship. I don't really want to be alone with him more than I am. I know that I'm called to serve him, and I want to fulfill that calling. I want God to bless and use my life. But I don't want to be more intimate with him than I am. He is like a boss I want to please but would rather not see after work.

You see, God has done things both in my life and in the world that I don't understand. He has chosen not to do things for me that I think he should have. I have serious questions about him and his dealings with men and women. Until I can find some resolution to these issues, it will be harder to trust him more than I do. I know that God's ways are higher than mine (Isaiah 55:9) and that there are mysteries humans cannot comprehend. But I want to try. If I must choose to accept God's ways by faith, I need to know that I did my best to understand them first.

Over the decades that I've been a pastor and across the years since he has led me to continue that calling through our work at Denison Ministries, I've been close enough to various people to share my questions about God with them. Without exception, the person I confided in has admitted that they have struggled with the same issues. Like me, the friend didn't feel secure in telling someone about doubts and frustrations. But when a professional Christian confesses his spiritual struggles, I guess others feel safer in admitting theirs.

So I'm writing this book for both of us. For you, in the hope that what you read will help you choose to trust God more than you do. But even more for myself, in the hope that I'll do the same. We'll see where we stand with God when this conversation ends.

ACKNOWLEDGMENTS

Unlike Jacob, I have not wrestled with God in solitude. Many people have given me wise counsel and gracious encouragement in the struggle.

The late Dr. Russell Dilday, former chancellor of B. H. Carroll Theological Institute and former president of Southwestern Baptist Theological Seminary, was a theological mentor and hero for decades. He was also the first to give me a platform from which to ask my questions. Faculty colleagues and gifted students in four graduate institutions have been my partners in the debate. Four of the greatest churches in America have allowed me to be their pastor and encouraged my quest for God. And through the work we're privileged to do at Denison Ministries, God has expanded both that platform and my calling to help others know and understand him better.

Vester Hughes was a spiritual father to me for many years. Dr. Gary Cook, chancellor of Dallas Baptist University and one of the finest leaders I know, has been my adviser and spiritual brother. Rev. Jeff Byrd has been my best friend and daily encourager. Our team members at Denison Ministries are amazingly gifted and vital partners in this calling.

Through a lifetime of questioning and wondering, my most constant source of hope has been my family. Our sons and their families are daily sources of joy. And Janet, my wife and life partner, is the wisest, most godly person I know, as well as my best friend. I dedicate this book to her, praying that it will glorify the God we will serve together forever.

INTRODUCTION

Wondering About God

For as long as I can remember, I have wondered about God. I have an early childhood memory of lying back in the cool grass in our front yard in Houston, Texas, and staring up at white, cottony clouds in the afternoon sky. *Where did they come from? Where did we come from? What is beyond this?* I thought there must be something on the other side of the sky I couldn't see, something surrounding the world that surrounded me. What I didn't know was where it all ended (or began). But I came to the reasoned, first-grade conclusion that the "something" must be God.

We didn't worship this God much in my family, or even talk about him. In fact, I don't remember having a real conversation about God with my parents or anyone else. I do remember finding out that my Cub Scout leader went to church on Wednesday nights, which meant our den had to meet on another night of the week. I asked my mother why anyone would go to church on Wednesday night. She didn't know.

Nothing changed until the ninth grade. I was in Mrs. Middleton's typing class, and she told us our typing would improve if we practiced typing whenever we could. For reasons I cannot begin to fathom, I wrote an "Essay to God." As far as I can recall, this was the first time I ever addressed him. I still have the essay, created on my father's World War II–era manual typewriter on lined, three-hole looseleaf paper.

I started the conversation on safe ground, telling God about my day (though it occurred to me as I sat typing that he would know more about it than I did). Then I got to the real issue, admitting that I wondered if he was real, and if he was, how could I know that he was? I now have an answer, but for a long time I didn't.

Do you ever wonder if the whole business of faith and religion isn't something we humans made up? If our belief in a heavenly Father is some Freudian wish projection? William James asked the question well: "Is the sense of Divine presence a sense of anything objectively true?"[1] If God is real, why hasn't he made himself so indisputably present that none of us need to wonder about this most crucial of all questions? And if he has, how has he done it?

This issue is front and center in today's culture, and doesn't appear to be going away anytime soon. So in *Wrestling with God*, we'll address it in two parts. The first section is about wrestling with skeptics—my attempt to show you why I believe that the God of the Bible is real and that Jesus is his Son. The second section moves on to the problems about which I'm not so certain, ones that I continue to wrestle with.

Is God Really Real?

One of the things I liked best about living in Dallas was the sunsets. There were no forests or mountains to get in the way of watching the sun go down. On a reasonably clear day you could see the sky change from blue to orange, purple, or red. I was never quite sure how much of it was natural and how much was caused by pollution, but either way, the experience was inspiring.

Of course, my God of the glowing sunset may be your God of the raging tsunami or life-taking hurricane. I say that God appeared to Abraham and did his work through Isaac and his descendants; Muslims say that he did the same thing through Ishmael and his heirs. I believe that God is a person; Hindus believe that *he* is an *it*, an impersonal reality. I can talk about all the ways I've been transformed by my faith, but Buddhists can say the same about their experiences on the path to enlightenment.

Who's to say who is right?

And what about all the horrors committed in God's name? This year marks the twenty-fifth anniversary of 9/11, and Americans still struggle to fathom how God could send his messengers to kill three thousand people in New York City. But Muslims cannot fathom how God could send his crusaders to annihilate Arabs for two centuries. Hitler was apparently egged on by anti-Semitic leaders, both Protestant and Catholic. Some people see suicide bombers as martyrs and view terrorist insurgents as freedom fighters. Whatever we call them, people are killing and being killed in the name of religion every day.

Is it time to admit that religion does more harm than good? Should we see the arguments about God's existence and nature, and the outrages performed in religious zeal, as evidence that God isn't real after all? Maybe we should agree with Freud that religion is nothing more than a childish wish fulfillment that we should all outgrow.

At the very least, why should we sacrifice our time, money, or service to a God whose existence and nature are so ambivalent? I might choose to go to church, to accept what I'm told, even to preach and teach the faith, believing that I'm doing more good than harm. But if God doesn't exist, is there something I can do with my life that is more reasonable or beneficial than what I'm doing right now? Why pay a price to be more intimate with a God whose very existence is uncertain to me? If we believe in the existence of God, the lordship of Christ, and the authority of Scripture, a skeptic would want to know why. Can we demonstrate with any rational certainty that the object of our faith is real? Or is our faith merely personal and subjective?

I suspect that many professing Christians have harbored similar questions. Could it be that we don't share God's story with others because we have our own doubts about him? Maybe Christians divorce at the same rate as the rest of the population and live in ways that are no different from the culture because we're not sure God is real enough to deserve what we are asked to sacrifice in obedience to him.

If we could be sure that God is real and the Bible is true, what would change about our lives and our churches? Would we mean the words of the hymns we sing? Would we actually do what the Bible says? Would we risk telling our neighbors about Jesus? If we modern-day Noahs were sure the flood was coming, would we build an ark of faith and invite everyone we know to get on board?

Billions of people say they believe in Jesus. How many have an intimate, transforming, obedient relationship with him? My guess is the same number as those who are sure he is who he says he is. Should we join their number? What difference will such a decision make in our lives?

What Exactly Is Faith?

Faith in God, like any other relationship, is a personal commitment. And all personal commitments transcend their evidence. Atheist Sam Harris claims:

> It is time we acknowledged a basic feature of human discourse: when considering the truth of a proposition, one is either engaged in an honest appraisal of the evidence and logical arguments, or one isn't. Religion is the one area of our lives where people imagine that some other standard of intellectual integrity applies.[2]

He could not be more wrong.

All personal relationships require a decision that goes beyond what evidence can prove. If I had waited until I was sure I would be a good husband, I would never have gotten married. If I had waited until I could prove I would be a good father, I would never have wanted children. In making relational choices, we should all be "engaged in an honest appraisal of the evidence and logical arguments." But then we must also be willing to recognize when those logical arguments have limits. Eventually, we have to step beyond the evidence into a commitment that becomes self-validating. You and I do this every day with every personal relationship in which we choose to trust or not to trust.

How we relate to God is no different. Harris complains that "faith is nothing more than the license religious people give one another to keep believing when reasons fail,"[3] but he's wrong. Christianity could easily be proven false *if* someone could prove that Jesus did not rise from the dead. And if that happens, "we are of all people most to be pitied" (1 Corinthians 15:19). If someone could prove that the Bible we read bears no trustworthy relationship to the original manuscripts of Scripture, we would be forced to abandon it as our authority source. As Christians, we examine the evidence and logical arguments, then step beyond them into the faith they support but cannot prove.

The atheist or agnostic does exactly the same thing, choosing to believe that there is no God or that he cannot be known. Neither of these conclusions can be proven beyond doubt. Christians in no sense seek "some other standard of intellectual integrity."

A Friend Who Changed My Mind

I hadn't planned to include chapters on the truth of Scripture, the existence of God, or the deity of Christ in this book. But then I spent an afternoon talking to a young man at our church's annual youth camp. His questions changed my mind.

He is a brilliant student, attending one of our nation's best universities on a math and science scholarship. He and my youngest son, Craig, have been friends for years. Our family has greatly admired this young man's gifts and his giving spirit. But I'd never had a long conversation with him before that afternoon. We talked very honestly about his faith questions: How do we know the Bible is true? How do we know that God is real or that Jesus is the Son of God? The answers he learned in Sunday school only confirmed his skepticism. He needed the best help I could give him.

I came away from that conversation convinced that there are more people with questions like my son's friend who are attending church camps and worship services. If you're wondering why you should believe the Bible, asking your question in the middle of a Sunday school class may not win friends. For example, I'd have to know a Muslim pretty well to ask why they believe the Qur'an without offending the person. If you're not sure you really believe in the existence of God or the deity of Christ, you may not know where to go to ask your questions. You can attend a local chapter of Atheists Anonymous (there really is a national organization by that name), but you probably won't get much objective help.

I hope that the first part of this book will be a safe place to explore such issues. Maybe you're reading it because you really do wonder whether you should trust the Bible, or because you want to investigate the existence of God and the deity of Christ.

Or it may be that you believe in all of the above, but aren't sure how you'd talk to my young friend at camp. Perhaps you'll find some answers here.

PART 1

Why Wrestle with God?

CHAPTER 1

Why Believe a Two-Thousand-Year-Old Book?

I'll never forget the evening I met Billy Graham. To be honest, I was more scared than excited. I was leading a delegation of preachers sent from churches in the Dallas–Fort Worth area to invite Dr. Graham to conduct a mission in our area. I was half certain that I'd say or do something to embarrass us all. As it turned out, I had every reason to be nervous.

Dr. Graham was speaking in Fresno, California, at the local university's football stadium. The locker room had been converted to a waiting area with chairs and tables. The world's most famous Christian was sitting there, waiting to go on the platform, when our little group of relative nobodies was ushered in to meet with him.

He had fallen the night before in his hotel room, breaking a bone in his foot. As we entered the locker room, we found Dr. Graham sitting in a red upholstered recliner, his injured foot in a walking cast propped up on a wooden coffee table. His sermon notes were open on his lap, a glass of water at his side. Even though it was a warm evening, he was wearing a sweater underneath his suit coat. At first glance I was struck by how frail he looked. Then he lifted his head and looked at us, and time stood still.

I've never seen such eyes. Blue, unwavering, gracious but piercing, kind but probing, seeing right into your soul. I'm sure that part of my reaction came from knowing Dr. Graham's reputation as one of the greatest evangelists since Paul. In that moment, I honestly felt myself to be in the holy presence of the Lord himself. During our thirty minutes together, as he turned those eyes to examine each of us individually, we all felt it. There was a power, a mystery, a convicting yet reassuring sense of divine presence in all he did and said. That night in the stadium, after he preached a brief, simple sermon, I watched in awe as thousands poured down from the stands onto the field to give themselves to Christ.

I lost count of the number of times Dr. Graham said, "The Bible says . . ." Quoting Scripture as his only authority, he captured the minds and souls of three generations gathered to hear him. Many wonder if there will be another like him. I don't think so.

I say that not just because of his unique charisma and godly passion, or his lifelong reputation for integrity. I'm skeptical that another Billy Graham will arise in this generation primarily because I don't think this culture really cares what the Bible says. We live in a world where the Qur'an, the Book of Mormon, the teachings of Buddha and of Hindu masters, and "wisdom" from the latest viral media clips compete with the Word of God for our attention. Our society doesn't believe in objective values or absolute truth. It's popular today to talk about your *personal* truth while respecting mine. "No one has the right to force their beliefs on me," people say. "'The Bible says' may be Billy Graham's truth or your truth, but that doesn't make it mine."

If I were a skeptic of Christianity, I would begin my argument with the Bible. I would try to convince you that it is a human rather than divine book, filled with contradictions and mistakes. If I could get you to abandon your trust in Scripture, I could remove most of the foundation upon which your faith is built. I'd try to persuade you that believing in the Bible is standing in quicksand. The longer you stay where you are, the lower you'll sink.

I wouldn't be the first person to attempt this strategy—not by a long shot.

Christopher Hitchens and Sam Harris

When I was growing up, our family Bible held a place of honor in the guest room. I was fascinated by this leather-bound book with its ribbon marker and pages edged with gold leaf. Our family tree—going back more than a century—was written down in beautiful calligraphy in the Bible's front pages. The whole thing was very mysterious to me.

The few times I had the nerve to actually read a little, I was put off by the *thee*s and *thou*s, and more than a little frightened by the pictures. A painting of David holding the severed head of Goliath was probably not the best way to introduce an eight-year-old to the grace of God. But it never would have occurred to me to question whether or not the Bible was true.

I'll bet most people of my generation felt the same way. Whether we read it or not, at least we didn't question that this book was inspired by the God of the universe. There certainly were no books at the local bookstore telling us that it wasn't.

How times have changed.

Christopher Hitchens was a former Marxist and stalwart atheist. His most famous work, *God Is Not Great,* was written for this purpose: "Dear reader, if you have come this far and found your own faith undermined—as I hope . . ."[4] In the book he concludes that "religion has run out of justifications. Thanks to the telescope and the microscope, it no longer offers any explanation of anything important."[5] I wish he'd told us what he really thought.

Since Hitchens rejected the Christian faith entirely, I was surprised when he disclosed in the book that (at his father's funeral) he quoted this passage from the Bible: "Finally, beloved, whatever is true, whatever is honorable, whatever is just, whatever is pure, whatever is pleasing, whatever is commendable, if there is any excellence and if there is anything worthy of praise, think about these things" (Philippians 4:8).[6]

But he quickly explained why: "I chose this because of its haunting and elusive character, which will be with me at the last hour, and for its essentially secular injunction, and because it shone out from the wasteland of rant and complaint and nonsense and bullying which surrounds it." (And to think that Philippians is my favorite book of the Bible.) Hitchens was no happier with the book of Revelation (my second favorite book) and its "deranged fantasies."[7] If Hitchens was right, any belief in God based on the Bible is wrongheaded and naive.

I wouldn't bother with Hitchens except that he speaks for a movement that helped to shape our present culture's reaction to religion. Aggressive atheism (as some called it) may not be as prominent now as it was fifteen years ago, but that is primarily because they simply don't have to be as aggressive anymore. Their call to relegate the Bible to the status of *The Odyssey* and *Paradise Lost*—interesting books of mythology, but nothing more—has become the accepted view of many outside of Christian circles and an alarming number of people who call themselves Christians as well. If you're wondering why you should trust the Bible, listening to Hitchens will give your questions a very loud voice.

Of course, Hitchens did not pretend to be an objective source for our conversation on the value of Scripture and faith. For instance, consider this kind and evenhanded statement: "Violent, irrational, intolerant, allied to racism and tribalism and bigotry, invested in ignorance and hostile to free inquiry, contemptuous of women and coercive toward children: organized religion ought to have a great deal on its conscience."[8]

Unfortunately, Hitchens's biases apparently got in the way of his research regarding the Bible. For instance, he claimed that "if Jesus was ever born, it wasn't until at least AD 4."[9] Considering that King Herod, the ruler who sought to kill the infant Jesus, died in 4 BC, Jesus's birth must have preceded that date. If you're interested in more erroneous attacks on Scripture by Hitchens, please consult the appendix.

Sam Harris, another prominent atheist author, is no more objective than Hitchens. As he writes in his *Letter to a Christian Nation,* "Atheism is nothing more than the noises reasonable people make in the presence of unjustified religious beliefs."[10] Apparently, he believes atheists are reasonable, yet people of faith are not.

However, Harris can mislead us on the facts as disastrously as Hitchens. For instance, he lists Jehovah's Witnesses as a "denomination of Christianity,"[11] a claim that is news to both Christians and Jehovah's Witnesses. And he states:

> The writers of Luke and Matthew, for instance, declare that Mary conceived as a virgin, relying upon the Greek rendering of Isaiah 7:14. The Hebrew text of Isaiah uses the word *'almâ*, however, which simply means "young woman," without any implication of virginity. It seems all but certain that the dogma of the virgin birth, and much of the Christian world's resulting anxiety about sex, was a product of a mistranslation from the Hebrew.[12]

If Harris had checked, he could have learned that Luke never quotes Isaiah 7:14. But why did Matthew? Because the Septuagint (the Greek Old Testament, translated by Hebrew scholars two centuries before the birth of Christ) rendered *'almâ* as *parthenos*, their word for *virgin*. In addition, Gabriel made it clear to Mary that she would be a virgin mother (Luke 1:34–36; note: no reference to Isaiah 7:14). The New Revised Standard Version renders Isaiah 7:14 as "young woman" and footnotes "virgin" as the Greek translation; the New Jerusalem Bible does the same. The Hebrew text is no secret kept from or by "the Christian world."

Harris is simply wrong in arguing that "the dogma of the virgin birth" is "a product of a mistranslation from the Hebrew." The appendix lists more mistreatments of Scripture by Harris and the obvious, often easy answers to his criticisms.

Hitchens and Harris do not bring a single criticism against the Bible that cannot be answered by the facts. If their skepticism was the only thing Christians had to answer, we'd be in good shape. Unfortunately, that is not the case.

Where Did We Get the Bible?

While Hitchens, Harris, and others in their movement dismiss the Bible as inaccurate, a far greater percentage of the population simply see it as irrelevant. The latter is a much graver accusation. So why should we believe the Bible is not only accurate in its teachings but relevant in its message? To begin, Christians have agreed that the Bible is the Word of God for nearly two thousand years.

The list of Old Testament books found in today's Bibles was finalized in the first century at two meetings of rabbis held at the city of Jamnia, a town west of Jerusalem near the Mediterranean coast. However, these meetings did not determine the books of the Hebrew Bible so much as they discussed and ratified what had been accepted by the Jewish people for centuries. The thirty-nine books of the Old Testament had even been translated into Greek two hundred years before these councils met.

And the process of codifying the New Testament was equally trustworthy.

Early Christians decided on four criteria for accepting a book as divinely inspired. First, it had to be written by an apostle or based on eyewitness testimony. Second, it had to possess obvious merit and authority. Third, a book had to be accepted by all Christians, not just a single church. Last, it had to be approved by the decision of the entire church, not just a few advocates.

Consider a book that didn't make the cut: *The First Gospel of the Infancy of Jesus Christ* tells of a man who was changed into a mule but converted back to human form when the baby Jesus was put on his back for a ride (7:5–27). The same book tells us that the infant Jesus killed some boys who made him angry (19:19–24). Sounds just like the Savior of the world, doesn't it? It was easy to dismiss such fiction.

The four gospels of our New Testament were chosen by AD 115, when Ignatius called them "the gospel." In AD 170, Tatian made a "harmony of the gospels" using only Matthew, Mark, Luke, and John. Around AD 180, Irenaeus referred to these four gospels as firmly established in the churches. The rest of the New Testament books were soon accepted by the entire church as well.[13]

F. F. Bruce was one of the world's most recognized authorities on the creation of the Bible. As he described:

> One thing must be emphatically stated. The New Testament books did not become authoritative for the Church because they were formally included in a canonical list; on the contrary, the Church included them in her canon because she already regarded them as divinely inspired, recognizing their innate worth and generally apostolic authority, direct or indirect. . . . What these councils did was not to impose something new upon the Christian communities but to codify what was already the general practice of those communities.[14]

Of course, we haven't proven that the Bible is the Word of God. But we have proven that its formation makes it one of the most well-sourced and historically reliable texts in existence. Moreover, it was produced by believers who claimed to be guided by the Spirit of God. Should we believe them?

Should We Trust the Bible?

Leigh Teabing, a central character in Dan Brown's *The Da Vinci Code*, epitomized the views of many who doubt the Bible's inspiration when he described it as "a product of *man*, my dear. Not of God. The Bible did not fall magically from the clouds. Man created it as a historical record of tumultuous times, and it has evolved through countless translations, additions, and revisions. History has never had a definitive version of the book."[15] Later he adds with a chuckle that scholars cannot confirm the authenticity of the Bible.[16]

What are the facts? Of course, the Bible claims to be the divinely inspired Word of God (John 10:35; Hebrews 4:12; 2 Timothy 3:16). But we would expect that. Is there objective historical evidence to support or refute this claim?

Biblical scholars consider four questions in determining the validity of an ancient book. First, has it been copied accurately across the centuries? This is the manuscript, or bibliographic, test. Second, what does archaeological evidence tell us? Third, is the book internally consistent? Fourth, if it makes predictions, are they fulfilled? While a full discussion of these issues requires a separate book, we can at least look briefly at the answers.[17]

First, let's consider the manuscript evidence. No original copies of any ancient book exist. The paper used by Aristotle, Plato, Julius Caesar, and the biblical writers was too fragile to last across the centuries. However, we possess five thousand copies of the New Testament in ancient Greek and ten thousand in other ancient languages. Some fragments were written thirty or so years after the original writings.

By contrast, we have only nine or ten good copies of Caesar's *The Gallic Wars*, none made earlier than nine hundred years after Caesar. For Tacitus's first-century *Histories* we have only four and a half of his original fourteen books, none copied earlier than the tenth century. We possess only five manuscripts of any work of Aristotle, none made earlier than AD 1100 (fourteen centuries after the original).

Manuscript evidence for the New Testament far surpasses the evidence for any other ancient book. Quoting F. F. Bruce again, "The variant readings about which any doubt remains among textual critics of the New Testament affect no material question of historic fact or of Christian faith and practice."[18] Any claim that history has never had a definitive version of the book is simply wrong.

Next let's look at the evidence of archaeology. Researchers continue to make discoveries that confirm the Bible. For instance, the pool of Beth-zada (Bethesda) described in John 5 was once dismissed as historical fiction. Then archaeologists located it in the northeast quarter of the Old City of Jerusalem. I've seen it myself.

Archaeologists have uncovered the remains of Caiaphas, the high priest during Jesus's trial and crucifixion. They unearthed the skeleton of Yohanan, a crucifixion victim from AD 70 whose remains confirm the details of Jesus's crucifixion as it is described in the Gospels. Archaeological evidence strongly supports the trustworthiness of Scripture.

Third, internal consistency is also important in deciding whether or not to trust a book. Taking the Gospels as an example, we find exactly the right kind of agreement. Each of the writers tells the story from his unique perspective, and yet they agree on every essential fact. When we interpret the biblical texts according to their intended meaning, so-called contradictions are always resolved.

For instance, a critic might say, "The Old Testament teaches, 'An eye for an eye and a tooth for a tooth.' But Jesus told us to turn the other cheek. Which is right?" Both. The

Old Testament command (Exodus 21:23–25) had to do with physical injury, limiting retribution to the actual crime. Jesus's statement (Matthew 5:38–39) had to do with insults, not bodily threats. He told us not to answer slander with slander; his teaching did not prohibit punishment for actual crimes. As another example, Matthew 4 records Jesus's temptations in this order: turn stones into bread (v. 3), jump from the temple (vv. 5–6), and worship Satan on a mountain (vv. 8–9). Luke 4 records the same temptations, but in a different order: turn stone to bread (v. 3), worship the devil on a mountain (vv. 5–7), and jump from the temple (vv. 9–11). Which is right?

In their intentional context, there is no contradiction. Neither Matthew nor Luke claimed to be writing historical chronology, so the order of Jesus's temptations was immaterial to their purpose. If two people ask you what you did yesterday, you can recount the events of your day in a different order to each person without contradicting yourself (unless you claim to be following strict chronology both times). So it is with this socalled contradiction in the Word of God. On occasion people will tell me that they don't believe the Bible because it is "filled with contradictions." I always ask them to name one. No one ever has.

Last, fulfilled prophecy is important in judging a book like the Bible. Probably the most important area of prophecy has to do with the Messiah, the one God promised to send to redeem his people. At least forty-eight major messianic prophecies can be found in the Old Testament. Jesus Christ fulfilled every one.

For instance, here are some of the prophecies that Jesus fulfilled in his crucifixion. I've listed only the prophecies that he could not have controlled himself:

A friend would betray him (Psalm 41:9; Matthew 10:4).

He would be sold for thirty pieces of silver (Zechariah 11:12; Matthew 26:15).

He would be wounded and bruised (Isaiah 53:5; Matthew 27:26).

He would be smitten and spit upon (Isaiah 50:6; Matthew 26:67).

He would be mocked (Psalm 22:7–8; Matthew 27:29).

His hands and feet would be pierced (Psalm 22:16; Luke 23:33).

He would be crucified with thieves (Isaiah 53:12; Matthew 27:38).

His garments were parted and lots cast for them (Psalm 22:18; John 19:23–24).

Not one of his bones would be broken (Exodus 12:46; John 19:33).

His side would be pierced (Zechariah 12:10; John 19:34).

He would be buried in a wealthy man's tomb (Isaiah 53:9; Matthew 27:57–60).

Of course, billions of people across twenty centuries of Christian history have proven the Bible to be true and relevant in their personal lives. But even if we discount such overwhelming subjective evidence, there are still compelling reasons to believe that the Bible is the trustworthy Word of God.

Should We Trust the Critics?

It's important for Christians to listen to the critics of Christianity. But we should also expect our critics to meet the same factual standards they expect of us. We've seen some of the mistakes made by Christopher Hitchens, Sam Harris, and Dan Brown.

In fact, discussing the historical errors in Dan Brown's novel could fill a short volume. Unfortunately, many of those errors have come to be accepted as facts in our culture today.

For instance, Brown calls the Nag Hammadi and Dead Sea Scrolls "the earliest Christian records."[19] But the Nag Hammadi library was written by Gnostics, heretics who were in no sense part of the Christian church. And the Dead Sea Scrolls contain *only* the Old Testament; their readers would be surprised to learn that they possessed "Christian records."

Brown claims that Noah was an albino,[20] but the Bible nowhere describes him this way. He describes Joseph of Arimathea as "Jesus's trusted uncle,"[21] but nothing in the Bible or early Christian history suggests this relationship.

We can view the Bible through the eyes of skeptics like Hitchens, Harris, and Brown, men who have no training in biblical study and interpretation but have a clear agenda to discredit the Christian faith. Or we can view their skepticism through the eyes of Scripture and those who have found God in its pages. I choose the latter.

So Should You Trust the Bible?

Has this chapter proven that the Bible is the inspired Word of God? Of course not. As I said in the introduction to part one, faith is a relationship, and relationships cannot be proven, only experienced. We cannot use scientific methods to prove relational truth any more than we can use a bathroom scale to measure friendship.

But we can consider the evidence that supports a relational decision. I couldn't prove that Janet would be a good wife until I married her, but I could examine the evidence before making my decision. Had she been in prison for attempting to murder her last boyfriend? Had she been divorced four times by her senior year of college? These issues might have been a deterrent. (I actually married so far above me that a friend who met my wife told me I had "outkicked my coverage.") Even if all the evidence was positive (and it was), I still couldn't be sure until we got married.

So it is with the Word of God. The evidence we've considered shows that trusting the Bible is reasonable. If we discovered that the Bible we read today bears no similarity to the original manuscripts, or that archaeology disproves Scripture, or that the books disagree with themselves, or that the Bible's prophecies are unfulfilled, we'd have reasons to reject the Bible as the Word of God.

In fact, the opposite is true. Rather than discovering vetoes to the Christian faith, we have found excellent evidence that it is based on a book we can trust. Now we must step beyond the evidence to experience—then the Bible becomes God's Word for us.

Of all the people I've known who have chosen to do that, one has stood out in my memory for many years. I met her during the summer of 1979 when I was working as a missionary in East Malaysia on the island of Borneo. Most of the Christians I encountered there had never owned a copy of the Bible in their own language. The mission team in Singapore sent my partner and me into the country with a large bag filled with paperback Malay New Testaments. They told us the Bibles would probably not get through customs, but that we should try. *Easy for you to say,* I thought to myself. *What if the Bibles are not the only things they take into custody?*

My partner and I came to the luggage checkpoint and placed our bags on the conveyor belt. The customs official zipped open our blue gym bag filled with New Testaments. I knew that only Muslims were allowed to work for the government, and I expected this Muslim to confiscate our bag or something worse. Instead, he zipped the bag shut, smiled at me, made a cross in the air, and sent it through.

But that's not the best part of the story. On Sunday we stood outside the small warehouse where the local Christian church met, ready to distribute our Bibles. The people formed a long line out into the dirt street. It was hot and humid in the tropical sun. Each person wanted to thank us for our gift. Their speeches and our responses to the hundred or so people waiting for their Bibles, all conveyed through our interpreter, took most of the afternoon.

Finally we came to the end of the line. An elderly woman, stooped over on her twisted cane, shuffled her way through the dust to our little table. I handed a New Testament to her. Her weathered hands trembled as she accepted the first Bible she had ever owned. She hugged it to her chest in a tight, loving embrace. Tears began to flow down her weathered cheeks. I thought of all the Bibles at home in my apartment gathering dust. And I was shamed by her love for the Word of God.

"The Bible says . . ." may not be all our culture wants to hear. But it's enough for God to say.

For Further Reflection

- Faith in God, like all relationships, requires a personal commitment transcending the evidence. Do you wish that faith could be more certain? Why or why not?
- Skeptics of biblical authority often allege that the Scriptures contradict themselves. Can you think of other motivations for their attacks on God's Word?
- As you have seen, the manuscript evidence for biblical authority is remarkable. What more could God have done to give us his Word in a way we would trust? Why do you think he transmitted the Bible to us as he did?
- How do you think a skeptic would respond to the evidence from fulfilled prophecy? How does this evidence relate to the definition of faith we've considered?
- Do you think that Christians often take the gift of God's Word for granted? Do you? What could be done to encourage greater reverence for Scripture?

CHAPTER 2

If God Is Real, Why Aren't We Sure?

I saw a church billboard once that caught my eye: "Since I don't believe in atheists, atheists don't exist." Growing up, it was pretty much that simple for me. The entire twenty-one years I lived in Houston, I never met anyone who admitted they were an atheist. Believing in God's existence was like believing in the solar system—it must be true, because everyone said it was. Or believing that there actually was a remarkable organ in my head that kept everything in my body going. I've never seen my brain, but I believe I have one.

Looking back, I'm glad an atheistic bully didn't kick sand on my faith, because I don't have any idea how I would have defended myself. Most people who believe in God today are probably like I was. That's what worries me most about the future of our faith today. When people create videos or publish books intended to talk us out of faith in God, they tend to go viral by appealing most to people who have never really thought in depth about whether God exists and, if he does, why that should matter.

So let's think about those questions. Obviously, it is hard to want a more intimate relationship with God if you're not sure he is real. It would be difficult to convince others that God exists if you're not convinced yourself. And it would be tough to explain your faith in God if you don't have good reasons why you believe in him.

The biblical writers presupposed the existence of God, as did their readers ("In the beginning, God . . ." Genesis 1:1). But this informal, unexamined belief doesn't satisfy those who question the reality of God. We cannot have a real relationship with people who do not exist except in our minds. We can have a dream, a hallucination, or a fantasy about them, but we'd be schizophrenic to spend much time communicating with or otherwise responding to our imaginary friends.

This is precisely what atheists claim—that God exists only as a dream, hallucination, or fantasy, a belief that cannot be proven or even defended rationally. The critics we met in the last chapter are as sure that God doesn't exist as they are certain that his Word isn't true.

Creation Without a Creator?

One way to respond to people who reject the existence of God is to ask how there can be a creation without a Creator. (This argument from cosmos to Creator is known to scholars as the *cosmological argument for God's existence.*) If the universe began as a big bang, where did the big bang come from? If you think life started as a cell floating in a pool of water, I want to know what or who made the water. Since we live in a world where every effect has a prior cause, it's easy for us to reason that the world came from somewhere or Someone. This *first cause* (to use Aristotle's term) we can call God.

Unfortunately for those of us who like this approach, it doesn't prove as much as we might think it does. For instance, scientists say that the universe is running down (the second law of thermodynamics). Someday, perhaps one hundred trillion trillion trillion years from now, all planets will cease to exist as energy is converted to matter. Everything will eventually collapse on itself. These cheery optimists call this happy day *heat death* and say that it will make the entire universe into one black hole. This is a rather pessimistic way of stating the law of thermodynamics. Skeptics then ask, Who's to say that this is not how the big bang started, using forces we still cannot understand? Or, looking at the universe another way, what if history moves as a circle rather than a line, with a succession of big bang expansions and contractions?

Skeptics cannot prove any of this, of course. But then neither can Christians prove our belief that God made the universe. The Bible obviously says that he did, and it predicts that he will one day turn history into eternity (2 Peter 3:10, Revelation 21:1–5). But it would be impossible to prove these claims unless we were there at the beginning or are there at the end. And using God's Word to prove God's existence is probably the dictionary definition of circular reasoning.

Design Without a Designer?

Another way to argue for God's existence begins with the design we see in our world. (Scholars call this the *teleological* argument, from the Greek *telos*, meaning *design* or *end*.) As I write these words, I'm sitting on a porch looking out over the beautiful hill country of Central Texas. I can see trees and grassy hills stretching to the horizon, none of them aware that I'm writing about them right now or caring much if I do. I can see why a skeptic might say that all of this beauty happened by natural processes.

But if I look from the horizon to the porch, I find sandstone brick pillars supporting a patio roof with ceiling fans chasing away the mud daubers. To my right is a swimming pool with its cleaning hose churning the water. I can't imagine that anyone would think that the sandstone bricks and roof and ceiling fans all just happened to be here, or that the pool just happened to exist. How much more complex is the world than a swimming pool?

Once we start down this mental path, we can find examples of remarkable design nearly everywhere we look. In a debate with the atheist Kai Nielsen, J. P. Moreland suggested several:

> In the formation of the universe, the balance of matter to antimatter had to be accurate to one part in ten billion for the universe to even arise. Had it been larger or greater by one part in ten billion, no universe would have arisen. There would also have been no universe capable of sustaining life if the

> expansion rate of the Big Bang had been one billionth of a percent larger or smaller.
>
> Furthermore, the chance possibilities of life arising spontaneously through mere chance has been calculated by Cambridge astronomer Fred Hoyle as being 1 in 10^{40}, which Hoyle likens to the probabilities of a tornado blowing through a junkyard and forming a Boeing 747. Had these values, these cosmic constants which are independent of one another, been infinitesimally greater or smaller than what they are, no life remotely similar to ours—indeed, no life at all—would have been possible.[22]

People who are persuaded by the design argument claim that the universe is not old enough for life to have evolved naturally. According to them, the odds that our present world could have evolved by random chance are too small to be plausible, if they're even possible. But there's a *but*, and it's a big one.

The easiest way for a skeptic to respond to this argument is to invoke Charles Darwin's assertion that life evolves through natural selection and survival of the fittest. If this is true, life did not come to exist as a tornado through a junkyard. Rather, we evolved through a process that chose the parts necessary to make that Boeing 747. The odds of random, or chance, occurrence are irrelevant in a world that evolved through such a process of selection.

Some evolutionists even claim that natural selection *must* have created life as we know it, that the odds were much higher in favor of life than against it. It would likely have taken much longer than fifteen billion years for the universe to have evolved through random coincidence, but this is not how things happened. According to evolutionists, natural selection sped up the process of creating life as we know it.

Scholars continue to debate the merits of Darwinian evolution. But whether you believe that Darwin was brilliant or deluded, you can see why atheistic evolutionists aren't too impressed with the design argument. If this is the best we can do, our skeptical friends will probably remain skeptical.

Morality Without a Moral God?

A third argument for God's existence begins with the fact of human morality. We all have a sense of right and wrong, but why? Where did your conscience come from? Your parents, you say. But where did your parents get theirs? And where did their parents get theirs? And so on. Ultimately we can reason back to a God who is holy and created the human race with a sense of morality that reflects his own.

Unfortunately, this approach is not very compelling for skeptics either. It's easy to claim that our morality illustrates the Darwinian principle of self-preservation, since it often does. (My wife told me when we got married that if I ever had an affair it wouldn't be a divorce that I needed to worry about, but a funeral. I believed her.) Or we could credit natural selection for encouraging morality as a way of ensuring the survival of the species.

Even moral choices that seem to violate the instinct for self-preservation, such as a Christian who dies for their faith, can be explained as a selfish quest for admiration in this life and glory in the next. A Muslim suicide bomber seeking reward in paradise illustrates the point tragically. I'm afraid our skeptical friends are still not impressed.

Reasons Not to Believe

It would seem that none of the classical arguments for God's existence can compel us to believe in him. What's worse, there are several reasons to reject such faith. First, as we have seen, evolutionary theory can be used to explain the design of the world apart from faith in a designing God.

Second, if there is actually a God who made all that exists, it would seem that we would know he is real. Harris makes an apparently reasonable statement: "An atheist is simply a person who believes that the 260 million Americans (87 percent of the population) claiming to 'never doubt the existence of God' should be obliged to present evidence for his existence."[23] It shouldn't be so hard to comply with his request.

Third, some atheists go so far as to claim that the very words *God exists* are meaningless and incoherent.[24] What do we mean by *God*? We cannot point to anything in the created world—since this would be idolatry—making creation into the Creator. Neither can we point to anything within the rational concept of God since by definition our finite minds cannot comprehend an infinite being. To say that God exists is like saying mumblefump exists. Since I just made up the word, and no one knows what it means (including me), my statement is incoherent. If we cannot speak rationally of God, how can we believe in him?

Fourth, the problem of innocent suffering greatly compounds things. As we will see in a later chapter, it's hard to believe that an all-loving, all-powerful God created a world filled with evil and suffering. As Harris points out, "An atheist is a person who believes that the murder of a single little girl—even once in a million years—casts doubt upon the idea of a benevolent God."[25] Of course it does.

Reasons to Believe

So where are we? One answer is to claim that God exists because the Bible says he does. Of course, that is the very definition of circular reasoning. The Qur'an claims that there is no God but Allah (the Arabic word for *God*) and that Muhammad is his prophet. The Book of Mormon, not surprisingly, supports the teachings of the Mormon Church. We'd be hard put to find a religion whose sacred writings do not advocate what the religion believes.

It helps that the Bible has such outstanding evidence for its trustworthy nature. But even considering the manuscripts, archaeological evidence, internal consistency, and fulfilled prophecy, we cannot prove that the Bible is *divinely* inspired or that the God it advocates actually exists.

A second response is to claim that it is reasonable to believe in God without trying to prove our assertion that he exists. While arguing from creation to Creator or design to Designer does not prove that God exists, such thinking is clearly logical. Skeptics may not agree that we are right, but they cannot prove that we are wrong. This fact is significant. It would obviously be a veto to the Christian faith if we could not demonstrate that believing in God is at least rational. I would have a hard time getting you to join me in worshipping Martians, since no evidence could persuade you of their existence (I hope). But we can argue logically that God made and designed the world. Even if skeptics credit evolutionary natural selection as the explanation for life as we know it, they cannot prove that they are right. Their theory may be plausible, but so is ours.

Once we have shown that believing in God is reasonable, we can invite people to step from evidence into experience. As with all relationships, a relationship with God becomes self-validating. I know that God exists because I have experienced him. His existence was reasonable before I met him, and it is personal now that I have.

A third way to argue for God's existence is to ask, What else do we want God to do to prove himself? How could he have done things differently? Consider the four attacks on his existence we noted earlier. The first was that evolutionists can point to natural selection as explaining life without a designing God. My hands typing these words could be seen as similar to a chimpanzee's hands peeling a banana. According to evolutionists, this fact proves that we come from a common ancestor. The adaptation of various species to their changing environments is further evidence of evolution at work, we're told. Similarity and adaptation show that the world could have evolved without God.

But consider the possibility that God made a world in which life can adapt to a changing environment. In that case, adaptation does not negate design—it proves it. Perhaps God wanted me to be able to type and a chimpanzee to be able to eat a banana, so he designed our hands in similar ways to perform similar functions. All cars have four wheels, but this doesn't mean that they all came from the same factory. God could have made a world without such similarities so evolutionists would have less evidence for their theory, but I'm glad my hands can type, even if a chimpanzee's hands could do the same.

The second attack on God's existence argued that if God made the universe, it is reasonable to assume that we would be sure of his existence. But how? What would we like God to do that he has not already done? He made a world that bears remarkable evidence of creative power and designing genius. Yes, we can explain life through adaptation, but that very adaptation is part of his brilliant plan.

God has stepped into his creation on numerous occasions. He sent his angels to men and women. He revealed himself in dreams and visions, and continues to do so today (as we will see in a later chapter). He entered the human race, folding omnipotence down into a fetus and becoming a man like us. He proved his divinity by rising from the grave and returning to heaven. He gave us a book that records these events in remarkable and trustworthy detail.

What more would we like him to do? He could appear to us as we read these words, just as he appeared in the flesh twenty centuries ago. But many did not believe in his divinity even when they saw his miracles and knew about his resurrection. In the same way, skeptics could dismiss our experience as a hallucination or dream, believing that our senses were deceiving us. The only way we could be absolutely certain that God exists would be to stand in his presence on judgment day. One day we all will.

Christianity can in fact be verified with absolute certainty. One day in the future we will be sure beyond any shadow of a doubt that God is real and Jesus is Lord. But God is graciously giving us another day to trust in him by faith, another day to step into a personal relationship with him and experience the verification that comes to those who meet God for themselves. One day time will run out, and every knee will bow and every tongue will confess that Jesus Christ is Lord, to the glory of God the Father (Philippians 2:10–11).

Until that day, there is nothing more a supernatural God can do to prove his existence through natural means. Asking the infinite, perfect God of the universe to prove himself to our finite, fallen minds is like asking him to make a square circle. It's not your fault if you cannot explain this chapter to your pet cat.

The third argument we noted earlier was that the statement "God exists" has no meaning or coherence, since we cannot define God through experience or reason. Again, how is this God's fault? What would we have him do differently? We should not be surprised that we cannot define or describe him through his creation. Or that our finite, fallen minds cannot understand or describe him through the use of reason.

If we could, he would not be God. If our brains were simple enough for us to understand them, we wouldn't be smart enough to understand them. How much more is this the case with the omnipotent Lord of the universe! As Mark

Twain purportedly said, "If I could understand every word of the Bible, I wouldn't believe that God wrote it."

The fourth argument against God's existence is the problem of innocent suffering. This tragic fact makes it understandably difficult for many to believe that an omnipotent, all-loving God exists. Later, we'll look at reasonable ways of responding to this challenge. In fact, we will discuss an approach that may make suffering an even greater cause for faith.

So Does God Exist?

Does the president of the United States or the king of England exist? Not so I can prove it personally. I can doubt every reference to them in the media. Maybe the king is dead and an actor is taking his place. Perhaps the president was killed by terrorists and a surrogate is playing his role for the sake of national security. Maybe their videos and speeches are AI generated. If you claim to have met them, I could refuse to believe you. After all, you might be in on the plot. Only if I met them for myself could I be absolutely certain that they are real.

Do love and friendship exist? I cannot prove to you that my wife loves me, or that my best friend is my best friend. I could tell you about the times they have expressed their commitment to me, but you could say they are lying. I could show you all the wonderful things they do for me, but you could claim that they are manipulating and misleading me. You'd have to experience my marriage or friendship to know that they are real. That's just the way it is with personal relationships, including a relationship with the God of the universe.

It seems to me that God has done everything he can do to prove his reality to us. The rational arguments for his existence demonstrate that faith is reasonable and logical. He has interacted with our world throughout human history and entered our human race personally. He gave us a trustworthy written record of his creative work. He is available personally to everyone who is willing to trust in him. As a result, you could argue that more evidence exists for God than for Julius Caesar or George Washington.

The biggest problem atheists have with believing in God is that such faith requires them to accept the supernatural. If I am a materialist, certain that supernatural reality cannot exist, no amount of proof or persuasion will convince me of a supernatural being. Once you conclude that the world must be flat, nothing in logic or experience can prove you wrong. The presupposition determines the conclusion.

Of course, believing that the supernatural cannot exist is in itself a belief. Materialism is a faith commitment. A materialist cannot prove that the supernatural does not exist any more than a supernaturalist can prove that it does. The best we can do is to examine the evidence and then make a decision that transcends it. You'll know God is real when you ask him to be real in your life.

It has been my privilege to travel frequently to Cuba over the years, speaking in Cuban churches and falling in love with the Cuban people. Cuban Christians are among the most gracious, joyous, and persecuted people I've ever known. When Cubans make their faith public and are baptized as Christians, everything changes. They are assigned to the worst jobs; their children get the hardest military assignments; their families are followed and harassed, and sometimes much worse. Such is life for a believer in a country whose government is officially atheistic.

Despite such daily opposition, the Christians I have met in Cuba worship God with passion and serve him with great delight. I've seen them stand for three hours in the heat of the summer, singing praises to the Lord. Some ride bikes or walk many miles to get to church services. They hold Bible studies in their homes and share their meager possessions with people even poorer than themselves. Their love for Jesus both shames and encourages me.

Baptism is an especially significant time for them. This is when they declare to the government and the world that they have decided to follow Jesus. This is when their society marks them as Christians and treats them accordingly. Baptism is their entrance into a world of constant persecution.

During one of my trips to Cuba, I was invited to participate in a mass baptism service. Despite the suffering these new Christians would face, more than a hundred new believers had decided to take this step of public obedience. The church's baptistery was not nearly large enough for the crowd, so we traveled by flatbed trucks and open buses to a lake on the outskirts of the town. Each of us who was baptizing waded out thirty or so feet into the shallow lake, then turned to face the crowd gathered along the bank.

Soon candidates began sloshing out to us. The first person I baptized was a young woman being carried through the water by a man I presumed to be her husband. I was surprised that she wasn't walking on her own; the lake wasn't very deep, so I assumed that she was afraid of the water. The man handed her to me. I took her in my arms, spoke the baptismal charge over her, and immersed her. When she came up out of the water, the joy on her face was beyond description. She shouted, "Hallelujah!" raising her arms victoriously into the air. I handed her back to her husband, who took her in his arms. When he did, he raised her up out of the lake. Then I saw that she had only one leg.

Surviving in her society with such a disability would be challenging enough for anyone. Doing so as a baptized Christian would make her life difficult beyond belief. But if you had seen her face and felt her joy, you wouldn't wonder for a moment if God was real in her life and soul. Or if he could be real in yours.

For Further Reflection

- How might skeptics answer the argument for God's existence from creation? How could a Christian respond?
- Some skeptics claim that the theory of evolution makes the design argument irrelevant. What do you think? Why?
- Human morality can be explained as an example of self-preservation. How would you defend the moral argument from this allegation?
- An atheist might ask how a Christian accounts for evil and suffering in the world. A Christian can counter by asking how an atheist accounts for good in a world without God. Do you think this response would be effective? Why or why not?
- Skeptics ask why we don't have proof that God exists. What more could God do to prove his existence to you today?

CHAPTER 3

If Christianity Is True, Why Aren't Christians Better People?

I'm not a big fan of bumper-sticker theology. The popular phrase "If you love Jesus, honk" seems trite to me. I'm waiting for the bumper sticker that reads: "If you love Jesus, tithe. Anyone can honk."

But I have seen a bumper sticker that impressed me. Its theology was simple: "Christians aren't perfect, just forgiven." I'm sure the person who created the slogan intended it as an antidote to the "holier than thou" reputation some Christians have earned in our society. But it's precisely the kind of thinking that skeptics love to hate. If Christianity is true, why aren't Christians better people than the rest of us? Or at least as good as the best of us?

Every time a famous Christian leader sins in public, I cringe. It happened again as I was writing this chapter. I'm sorry for the man who has had to admit his crime to the world, his wife and children whom he has hurt, and the church and ministry he has devastated. But I'm also angry because I know that somewhere there are critics of the Christian faith smiling smugly and claiming yet another reason for their skepticism. The worst part is that their reaction is completely understandable.

If a diet guru ends up in the hospital with obesity-related diabetes, not many of us will buy his books. You don't want your bank teller to be suffering from dyslexia or your tax preparer to be indicted for tax fraud. A reasonable way to choose a new car is to talk to people who bought the same kind of car. Your experience will probably be similar to theirs.

Jesus said that he came to give us life *abundantly* (John 10:10). He taught his followers to "be perfect, therefore, as your heavenly Father is perfect" (Matthew 5:48 NIV). We are told that "sexual immorality and impurity of any kind or greed must not even be mentioned among you, as is proper among saints" (Ephesians 5:3 NRSVUE). Jesus called his followers the "light of the world" (Matthew 5:14) and expects us to reflect his light in everything we do.

Then why aren't Christians more like Christ? It would be hard to want a more intimate relationship with God if this relationship didn't make any real difference in your life or world. Many critics of Christianity are convinced that it doesn't.

Is Religion Immoral?

Christopher Hitchens spoke for many atheists when he described the ethics of religion:

> We believe with certainty that an ethical life can be lived without religion. And we know for a fact that the corollary holds true—that religion has caused innumerable people not just to conduct themselves no better than others, but to award themselves permission to behave in ways that would make a brothel-keeper or an ethnic cleanser raise an eyebrow.[26]

He later adds, "As I write these words, and as you read them, people of faith are in their different ways planning your and my destruction, and the destruction of all the hard-won human attainments that I have touched upon. *Religion poisons everything.*"[27] Hitchens is convinced that "ethics and morality are quite independent of faith, and cannot be derived from it," and that as a result, "religion is—because it claims a special divine exemption for its practices and beliefs—not just amoral but immoral."[28]

Fellow atheist author Sam Harris adds his view:

> One of the most pernicious effects of religion is that it tends to divorce morality from the reality of human and animal suffering. Religion allows people to imagine that their concerns are moral when they are not—that is, when they have nothing to do with suffering or its alleviation. . . . This explains why Christians like yourself expend more "moral" energy opposing abortion than fighting genocide. It explains why you are more concerned about

> human embryos than about the lifesaving promise of stem-cell research. And it explains why you can preach against condom use in sub-Saharan Africa while millions die from AIDS there each year.[29]

Harris then directs his ire at those who oppose abortion for religious reasons:

> If it is acceptable to treat a person whose brain has died as something less than a human being, it should be acceptable to treat a blastocyst as such. If you are concerned about suffering in this universe, killing a fly should present you with greater moral difficulties than killing a human blastocyst.[30]

Suppose we defend the blastocyst, since it has the potential to become a fully developed human being. Harris is ready for us:

> Almost every cell in your body is a potential human being, given our recent advances in genetic engineering. Every time you scratch your nose, you have committed a Holocaust of potential human beings. This is a fact. The argument from a cell's potential gets you absolutely nowhere.[31]

I cannot help interjecting a question here. If carried to term, a blastocyst will become a human being. Will the cells on my nose? Because of their opposition to abortion, many

Christians also oppose the use of aborted fetuses for stem-cell research. Harris is convinced that "your beliefs about the human soul are, at this very moment, prolonging the scarcely endurable misery of tens of millions of human beings."[32] Yet stem-cell research is years—if not decades—away from producing tangible benefits for humans. Even if researchers received all the funds they request, they admit that it will take years of experimentation to produce any genuine advances.

Harris next claims that atheists are more moral than religious people, citing the Muslim riots over Danish cartoons as evidence. He asks, "When was the last atheist riot?"[33] We might point to Hitler, Stalin, Mao Zedong, Pol Pot, and Kim Il Sung as less-than-stellar representatives of atheism, but Harris dismisses our claim since "they are never especially rational."[34]

Now Harris turns up the heat: "The fifty nations now ranked lowest in terms of the United Nations' human development index are unwaveringly religious."[35] He admits that there is no way to prove that religion causes poverty, but he is nonetheless sure that "atheism is compatible with the basic aspirations of a civil society" and that "widespread belief in God does not ensure a society's health."[36]

So he concludes: "Once you stop swaddling the reality of the world's suffering in religious fantasies, you will feel in your bones just how precious life is—and, indeed, how unfortunate it is that millions of human beings suffer the most harrowing abridgements of their happiness for no good reason at all."[37]

I can see why Hitchens and Harris are atheists. If I believed what they believe, I probably would be too.

Confusing Religion with Religions

In a moment we'll look at reasons why becoming a Christian is the most ethical thing you can do. But first, we need to take a closer look at the devastating criticisms we've just read.

Notice how these skeptics paint all religions with the same brush. Hitchens again spoke for many when he asserted that "religion has caused innumerable people not just to conduct themselves no better than others, but to award themselves permission to behave in ways that would make a brothel-keeper or an ethnic cleanser raise an eyebrow."[38] Which religion? Are we supposed to blame Islam for the moral failures of Hindus, or Christians for the immorality of emperor-worshipping Romans?

We are told that "people of faith are in their different ways planning your and my destruction."[39] Which people of faith? I assume he means Islamic jihadists. I don't even blame Islam for the horrors caused by these terrorists, much less my Jewish neighbor.

Harris states that "the fifty nations now ranked lowest in terms of the United Nations' human development index are unwaveringly religious."[40] Which religions do they follow? How is their religion in any way related to their socioeconomic status? Could it be that their faith helps them cope with crushing poverty rather than causing it?

It is typical for critics of a movement to find the worst of its followers, then claim that they represent everyone who shares their beliefs. Christianity still suffers in the Middle East from the horrific sins of the Crusades, as our enemies claim that all Christians supported these papal wars and would do so again. In recent years, the Roman Catholic Church has been dealing with a public relations disaster caused by the reprehensible sins of some of its priests.

But as unfair as these attacks may be, at least they do not blame an organization for offenses none of its members committed. To criticize golfers for the steroids abuse scandal in baseball makes no sense. To blame all Arabs for 9/11 is tragically absurd. To blame all religions for the moral failures of some religious people is like blaming all Brits for the sinking of the Titanic. Such rhetoric generates far more heat than light.

Confusing Morality with Health

Next, see how antagonists like Hitchens and Harris confuse morality with the prevention of suffering. Harris makes this connection clear when he complains that "religion allows people to imagine that their concerns are moral when they are not—that is, when they have nothing to do with suffering or its alleviation."[41] So we should fight genocide, not abortion; we should promote stem-cell research, not the defense of embryos; we should promote condoms to prevent AIDS rather than worrying about sexual immorality.

This is a common complaint against Christians who oppose abortion, stand against the legalization of marijuana or prostitution, or promote any other biblical moral standard. In a culture that believes that all ethics are relative and personal, preventing suffering is probably the best moral position they can promote. But consider their argument on its own merits.

When alleviating suffering becomes our highest moral priority, will we stop with the use of defenseless embryos and the promotion of condoms? Euthanasia becomes an obvious next step. And not just for those in the last stages of a terminal disease. By this logic, if suffering is our enemy, then anyone in pain should be able to end their lives if they wish. Canada has expanded their medical assistance in dying program under just this reasoning, with other countries considering the same.

What if children decide that their parents have caused them emotional suffering? They should divorce them, as some are already trying to do. (Never mind the emotional suffering parents would experience as a result.) What if a pastor makes a statement in a sermon that is considered offensive by a homosexual? Legislation that has come perilously close to passing on several occasions could make such speech a hate crime.

By contrast, the objective ethics found in the Bible speak to both the causes and the symptoms of human suffering. Imagine a world without murder, adultery, theft, lying, or coveting (Exodus 20:13–17). Imagine a society where we forgive those who hurt us rather than seeking revenge (Matthew 5:38–42), where the strong support the weak (Romans 15:1) and the rich help the poor (Acts 4:32–37). If someone asks whether I'd rather have a painkiller for my migraine or take medicine that will eventually end all headaches, I'd answer yes—to both.

Confusing Good with Godly

Critics of religion like to claim that atheists often live better lives than religious people. For instance, we read Harris's claim that "atheism is compatible with the basic aspirations of a civil society" while "widespread belief in God does not ensure a society's health." Since atheists do not often riot over offensive cartoons, they must be at least morally equivalent to religious people, if not superior to them.

As with their other attacks, Hitchens and Harris have once again spoken for many. If you can be as moral and happy as me without following Christ, why should you follow him? This argument shows that "good people" are often the hardest to convince that they should consider the claims of Jesus.

I can understand where they are coming from. If I am enjoying good health today, I will probably see no need to have an annual physical exam just because you tell me I should. I might even claim that the practice of medicine is mostly fraudulent. "Sure," I'd respond, "doctors help some people, but look at all the sick patients they cannot help because of the money they charge. Do you really want to support the bloated pharmaceutical industry? Do you realize that doctors suffer from the same problems that they claim they can alleviate in others?"

But there are holes in my logic. Perhaps there is a level of health I have never known but that I could experience—available only to people who see a doctor regularly. Perhaps I am threatened with a contagious disease that I do not know exists and need a vaccination that I am not aware I need. Perhaps my good health does not result from medical abstinence but merely from good genetics and lucky circumstances.

This is the position of "good people" who refuse to follow Christ. They think they are happy, but they have never experienced the joy that Jesus gives. They are facing a death and eternity for which their moral efforts cannot prepare them. They are convinced that they live good lives without God, when in fact they are the product of circumstances blessed by God.

If you are thinking that your personal morality means you don't need a relationship with God, I need to ask you: Did you deserve to be born in relative prosperity rather than abject poverty and the crime it breeds? If you were born to loving parents rather than abusive parents, did you earn that right?

The truth is that I can go only so long without consulting my family doctor. One day I'll get sick, no matter how proud I am of my health today.

Confusing Religion with Faith

Our critics want religion to make the world better before they'll believe it is worth their consideration. However, Christianity is not a prosperity religion but a personal relationship. It never claimed to transform the socioeconomics of a nation where its followers live or to guarantee health and wealth to people. In fact, the Bible often warns us of the opposite. Jesus cautioned us that "in the world you face persecution" (John 16:33 NRSVUE). Paul told us that "it is through many persecutions that we must enter the kingdom of God" (Acts 14:22 NRSVUE). Jesus suffered a horrible death, all but one of his apostles was martyred, and more than a million Christians were killed by the Roman Empire for no crime except following Jesus.

Nowhere does Scripture say that Christianity will make a country healthier or wealthier. Measuring our faith by the socioeconomics of nations where we live is like blaming

Mexican immigrants for global warming in Texas or Bourbon Street parties for the devastation of hurricanes.

Conversely, the fact that Christianity has grown exponentially despite persecution is one of the strongest reasons to believe that it does what it claims to do. Not long ago I was talking with a very bright graduate student about this very subject. She wanted to know why I believed that the God of the Bible is the true God of the universe. As I thought out loud with her, I heard myself say, "Because Christianity cannot be explained any other way." I'd never thought about that idea before. But the more I unpacked it for her, the more I became convinced of its truth. Here's what I said:

Hinduism, Buddhism, and Islam were birthed in circumstances that were conducive to their survival and growth. For instance, there were excellent economic and personal reasons for people living on the Arabian peninsula to join the growing Muslim movement. As Islam spread through military means across the decadent medieval European landscape, its growth could be expected and explained. Likewise, Hindus and Buddhists do not typically suffer great persecution for following their beliefs. While early Mormons and Jehovah's Witnesses often faced ridicule for their beliefs, none were crucified for them. They have grown in numbers as they have grown in acceptance by American society.

But Judaism and Christianity have survived and grown over the centuries despite horrific persecution and opposition. The Hebrew people lived through four centuries of Egyptian slavery and Judaism has persisted for four millennia despite the most systematic genocides ever attempted. Early Christians were crucified and massacred by the millions for refusing to worship Caesar. I have visited some of the catacombs of Rome, where a quarter of a million Christians were buried, many of them killed for their faith.

The first disciples had no self-serving reasons whatsoever for following their crucified Master. They faced inevitable torture and death for preaching his gospel. Their movement grew despite every effort of the mightiest empire in world history to exterminate its followers. In the centuries to follow, the Christian faith has most often been strongest where its opponents have been most antagonistic.

For example, when Christian missionaries were forced out of China following the communist takeover there, many predicted that the Chinese church would die. Instead, Chinese Christianity has grown ten-thousandfold. As many as twenty thousand people a day choose to follow Jesus in a country whose government is officially atheistic.

In the last chapter I mentioned my trips to Cuba. I can testify personally to the remarkable strength of the Christian church on an island whose government has done all it can to oppose the gospel. Churches cannot own buildings unless they owned their property prior to the Castro revolution in the late 1950s. Congregations must often wait several years for permission to spend building funds they already possess. Christian leaders face scrutiny and often imprisonment for their faith. And yet the Christian movement in Cuba is the strongest it has been in the history of the nation.

Does the sacrificial strength of the Christian faith prove its validity? Not for everyone. As we have seen throughout this book, it is impossible to use natural means to prove supernatural reality. There are always other ways to explain an event or movement.

For instance, a skeptic can claim that Christian martyrs are not unique, as Islamic suicide bombers are equally willing to die for their faith. But jihadists are taught that dying as a martyr is the only way to be certain they will go to paradise and receive eternal reward. By contrast, Christian martyrs do not seek death as a way to heaven, since they are already sure that Jesus has given them eternal life. Rather, they accept suffering as a consequence of following their Lord. And many have refused to recant their faith even when their family members were tortured and massacred as a result.

I suppose a critic could explain the growth of Christianity in the face of suffering by arguing that many believers have little to live for on earth and a glorious paradise awaits them after death. These believers have little to lose if they follow Jesus. But this claim does not explain the readiness of successful first-century businessmen like Peter, Andrew, James, John, and Matthew to suffer and die for Christ, or the willingness of a prosperous Saul of Tarsus to lose all things for Jesus (Philippians 3:1–11). It does not tell us why thousands of Cubans would willingly lose relative prosperity rather than deny Jesus. Or why millions of Chinese Christians would follow Christ in the face of threatened imprisonment, exile, or death. In each example, the people who followed Christ were willing to lose everything.

Quite frankly, I do not know of another religious movement that has grown as much as Christianity has in the face of merciless persecution. Or of a naturalistic explanation for this fact. People do not generally die for a lie, yet the first Christians lived in a time close enough to Jesus's death and resurrection to know the truthfulness of the gospel. From then to now, Christianity has become the largest spiritual movement in human history despite global opposition.

And Christians have demonstrated the reality of their faith by praying for the very people who persecuted them. Jesus set the example when he prayed for the soldiers who crucified him (Luke 23:34). Paul saved the life of his Philippian jailer and led him to eternal life in Christ (Acts 16:25–34). Peter told his readers to honor the very authorities who were oppressing them (1 Peter 2:17). Early tradition says that when John was jailed on Patmos, he led his jailers to Christ and started a church that still worships Jesus on the island today.

I know Cuban Christians who pray every day for God to bring their atheistic government leaders to faith in Jesus and to make them prosperous. I know suffering believers in Muslim lands who have forgiven their persecutors and pray daily for their souls. Skeptics who ask why Christians aren't better people don't know some of the forgiving, grace-giving believers I've met around the world.

Is It Ethical to Be Religious?

In a *Newsweek* conversation with Sam Harris, pastor Rick Warren once said that he never met an atheist who wasn't angry. Mr. Harris replied, "Let me be the first." To which Warren replied, "I think your books are quite angry."[42]

Here's a reason why Warren might have thought so. In his conclusion Harris claims,

> As a biological phenomenon, religion is the product of cognitive processes that have deep roots in our evolutionary past. Some researchers have speculated that religion itself may have played an important role in getting large groups of prehistoric humans to socially cohere. If this is true, we can say that religion has served an important purpose. This does not suggest, however, that it serves an important purpose *now*. There is, after all, nothing more natural than rape. But no one would argue that rape is good, or compatible with a civil society, because it may have had evolutionary advantages for our ancestors. That religion may have served some necessary function for us in the past does not preclude the possibility that it is now the greatest impediment to our building a global civilization.[43]

I have never before seen religion compared to rape. Could Harris have chosen a more unfortunate slander?

I do not wish to respond in kind. A person who does not believe in God is not by definition immoral or irrational. I understand why an Auschwitz survivor would wonder how God could be real, or why a father losing a child could question God's existence. My greatest fear as a father is that something might happen to my two sons. If a doctor were to tell me that one of them has terminal cancer, my first thought would be, *Why, God?* My second thought might well be, *Is there a God?* If Jesus could cry out on the cross to a God who seemed absent to him, we should not be surprised when we feel the same way.

Fortunately, the existence of God is based on facts, not feelings. It is a fact that the Bible is the best-attested ancient book in history. Its manuscripts, archaeological evidence, internal consistency, and fulfilled prophecies show that it is trustworthy and reliable. Evidence for a creating, designing, moral God is clear, though no natural evidence can be 100 percent conclusive for a supernatural reality.

At the end of the day, a relationship with God is like every other relationship. You chose to have a reading relationship with me through this book, though no evidence could prove that you should. A friend might have recommended my book, but that's no guarantee you'll read it. You might thumb through its pages, but you can't always tell a book by its chapter titles. You'd have to read this book to know with absolute certainty if you should read this book.

So it is with God. I can tell you that you should trust in Christ as your Lord, but I cannot prove to you why you should. If you've been to Niagara Falls or seen a sunset over the Grand Canyon, you can try to describe them to me. But you'll probably struggle with words, finally giving up and saying, "You'd just have to see it for yourself." That's how I feel about experiencing God.

I hope that you believe that your Creator is real and that his Word is reliable. Reason and evidence both warrant such a conclusion and commitment. If you are not a believer, I hope you'll take the leap of faith into a relationship with God you cannot prove rationally but can experience personally. If you do, you'll find that you've jumped not into the dark but into the light. I know because that's what happened for me.

My father's death during my senior year of college was and still is the great tragedy of my life. That first night after he was gone, I went out into the backyard of my parents' home, stared up into the black sky, and actually shook my fist at God. But thankfully he did not shake his fist back at me. Instead, he offered me his hand. Once again I discovered that the God of the Bible is real, because he was real to me when I needed him most. He sent friends to share my hurt, his Word spoke to my heart, and prayer became more intimate. His comfort and encouragement during the darkest days of my life were proof that he is present when we need him most.

With God, it's not true that seeing is believing. Rather, believing is seeing.

For Further Reflection

- Why do you think skeptics often confuse Christianity with other world religions? How does this confusion advance their argument?
- Good people who refuse to trust in God often claim that they don't need religion to be moral. How would you respond to them?
- This chapter argues that Christianity's growth in the face of persecution is strong evidence for its truth and relevance. Do you agree or disagree? Why?
- How would you assess the claim that faith in God is a relationship that cannot be proven, only experienced?

CHAPTER 4

Is Jesus Really God?

Why should you believe that Jesus is God? No other religion does. What makes Christians right and everyone else wrong?

You might believe that the Bible is trustworthy, that God exists, and that being a Christian is a moral choice to make. But none of these decisions mean that Christians are right about Jesus. If we're wrong about him, the central belief of our faith is wrong. If Muslims were proven wrong about Mohammed or Buddhists about Buddha, we wouldn't be very impressed with their religion. Likewise, it would be difficult to want a more intimate relationship with God through Christ if you weren't sure who Christ is. So why should you believe that Christians are right about the divinity of Jesus?

I remember vividly the day when I first had to answer that question for myself.

In college I was given a book on evidences for the Christian faith, and I read through it with mild interest. I was busy as a student and church youth minister, happy with my life and friends. I had all the faith I wanted, and all the faith I thought I needed.

That all changed during the spring semester of my senior year. I was at a college retreat, planning to graduate in a few months and attend seminary in the fall. Janet and I were engaged to be married and planning a life of church work together. On the Saturday morning of the retreat, I woke up with doubts I had never verbalized before. Did I really want to give the rest of my life to this? Was I absolutely sure that Christianity was true? Was it more than Sunday school lessons and sermons preached by paid Christians? Was preaching and teaching this faith worth my life and future?

I went for a long walk in the woods. I can still remember the blue sky through the pine trees that day and the crunch of the leaves and pine needles beneath my tennis shoes. I was gone for hours, reviewing in my mind what I had read in that book on the evidences for Christianity and thinking about the intellectual foundations of the faith. When I came back, I was convinced that Jesus is the Son of God and that sharing his gospel was worth my life. I still am. The contents of this chapter explain the reasons.

Perhaps you are in the place where I was. You may believe that God exists and that the Bible has been transmitted accurately, but you need reasons to be sure that Jesus is really the divine Son of God. The New Testament says that he is, but the Qur'an teaches that Allah is the only God. Jews, Buddhists, and Hindus have no interest in worshipping Jesus and have their own sacred writings to support their traditions. Do we have any evidence besides the New Testament to support our belief that Jesus is the King of Kings?

And what do we do with the claim that the doctrine of Jesus's divinity evolved centuries after his life and death? If we're not sure that Jesus is Lord, why would we pay a sacrificial price to know him better or tell someone else about him?

Perhaps you are certain that Jesus is God. How would you convince me that he is? Skeptics won't be impressed with the fact that you believe in Jesus because you believe the Bible. They'd call your faith circular reasoning, and they'd be right. You can tell them what Jesus has done for you, but they can point to the spiritual experiences of Muslims, Buddhists, and Hindus.

The good news is that even without the New Testament, the evidence for the divinity of Jesus Christ is amazing. Let's look briefly at the facts that persuaded me on that Saturday morning so long ago. Perhaps they'll do the same for you.

Is There Non-Christian Evidence for Jesus?

If Jesus is really God, it would seem that we wouldn't need the New Testament to tell us so. Non-Christians who wrote during the early years of the Christian movement surely would know something about him. And in fact, they did.

If I refused to open a New Testament, what could you tell me about Jesus? Everything I'd need to know to trust in him as my Lord. If we had no New Testament, we could defend the belief that Jesus is Lord solely on the basis of non-Christian writings nearly all as old as the New Testament books themselves. Here is a brief survey of the evidence, presented in chronological order.

Thallus the Samaritan (AD 52) wrote a work tracing the history of Greece from the Trojan War to his own day. In it he attempted to explain the darkness during the crucifixion of Jesus as an eclipse of the sun. This is the earliest pagan reference to Jesus's existence and death.

Mara bar-Serapion (writing after AD 70, as he describes the fall of Jerusalem) adds: "What advantage did the Jews gain from executing their wise King? It was just after that their kingdom was abolished."[44] His letter is on display in the British Museum today. It shows that the first Christians saw Jesus not just as a religious teacher, but as their King.

The Roman historian Suetonius (AD 65–135) records, "Punishment was inflicted on the Christians, a class of men given to a new and mischievous superstition."[45] Note that the empire would not punish people who followed a religious teacher, only those who made him Lord in place of Caesar.

Tacitus (AD 55–120) was the greatest ancient Roman historian. Around AD 115 he wrote, "Christus . . . suffered the extreme penalty during the reign of Tiberius at the hands of one of our procurators, Pontius Pilatus, and a most mischievous superstition broke out."[46] His description of the Christian faith as "superstition" shows that Tacitus considered the followers of Christus to believe something supernatural or miraculous, not simply that Jesus was a great human teacher. And it proves the New Testament record that Jesus was crucified by Pontius Pilate.

Pliny the Younger was a Roman administrator, author, and governor of Bithynia in Asia Minor. Two volumes of his letters are in existence today. The tenth of his correspondence books (written around AD 112) contains the earliest nonbiblical description of Christian worship: "They were in the habit of meeting on a certain fixed day before it was light, when they sang in alternate verses a hymn to Christ as to a god."[47] Note that believers worshipped Christ as God in AD 112, not centuries later after their beliefs evolved, as some critics claim.

Flavius Josephus, the noted Jewish historian (ca. AD 37–97), records that Ananias, "assembled the Sanhedrim of the judges, and brought before them the brother of Jesus, who was called Christ, whose name was James, and some others . . . and when he had formed an accusation against them as breakers of the law, he delivered them to be stoned."[48] Thus the Christians called Jesus the Christ, the Messiah.

Finally, consider Josephus's most famous statement about Jesus:

> Now, there was about this time, Jesus, a wise man, if it be lawful to call him a man, for he was a doer of wonderful works, a teacher of such men as receive the truth with pleasure. He drew over to him both many of the Jews, and many of the Gentiles. He was Christ; and when Pilate, at the suggestion of the principal men amongst us, had condemned him to the cross, those that loved him at the first did not forsake him, for he appeared to them alive again the third day, as the divine prophets

> had foretold these and ten thousand other wonderful things concerning him; and the tribe of Christians, so named from him, are not extinct at this day.[49]

While most historians do not believe that this paragraph represents Josephus's own faith, it does document the beliefs of early Christians regarding Jesus—an observation Josephus recorded before the end of the first century.

So from these early non-Christian records we know that Jesus Christ existed, that he was crucified, and that the first Christians believed he was raised from the dead and worshipped him as Lord. These are the facts of the gospel. And we can be sure of them without opening a Bible.

What Did the Earliest Christians Believe?

Let's think some more about the claim that the divinity of Jesus was developed by the church over centuries. In addition to the nonbiblical evidence we've just considered, it is easy to know what early Christians thought of Jesus. His earliest followers would be shocked to hear the accusation that the church transformed the earthly Jesus into the divine Christ.

For instance, The Didache (written before AD 100) repeatedly called Jesus "the Lord." It ends with "The Lord shall come and all his saints with him. Then shall the world 'see the Lord coming on the clouds of Heaven.'"[50] Clement of Rome, writing in AD 95, repeatedly referred to the "Lord Jesus Christ." And he promised a "future resurrection," which God will produce on the basis of his "raising Him from the dead."

Ignatius, writing between AD 110 and 115, referred to "Jesus Christ our God" in his introduction to the book of Ephesians.[51] To the Smyrnaeans he added, "I give glory to Jesus Christ, the God who has thus given you wisdom."[52] And Justin the Martyr (ca. AD 150) repeatedly referred to Jesus as the Son of God.[53] He was convinced that God raised Jesus from the dead and brought him to heaven.[54]

The Roman Empire would have considered followers of a mere rabbi to be no threat to its power. And yet it persecuted and executed Christians. Why? Because they claimed no king but the Lord Jesus. The radical faith and courage of the first apostles and the rapid spread of the Christian movement cannot be explained except by the fact that the living Lord Jesus changed their lives and empowered their witness. Thousands upon thousands died because of their commitment to him. And people don't die for what they know to be a lie.

Did Jesus Claim to Be God?

In recent years many skeptics have claimed that Jesus of Nazareth saw himself only as a religious teacher, and that the church deified him over the centuries. Not according to the eyewitnesses. When Jesus stood on trial for his life, the high priest challenged him: "I put you under oath before the living God, tell us if you are the Messiah, the Son of God" (Matthew 26:63 NRSVUE). His answer sealed his fate: "You have said so" (Matthew 26:64). Earlier he told his opponents, "Before Abraham was, I am" (John 8:58). He clearly claimed to be God.

The Gospels record further evidence in Jesus's own words:

> Heaven and earth will pass away, but my words will not pass away. (Matthew 24:35)

> "So that you may know that the Son of Man has authority on earth to forgive sins"—he said to the paralytic—"I say to you, stand up, take your mat, and go to your home." And he stood up and immediately took the mat and went out before all of them, so that they were all amazed and glorified God, saying, "We have never seen anything like this!" (Mark 2:10–12 NRSVUE)

> Anyone who does not honor the Son does not honor the Father who sent him. (John 5:23 NRSVUE)

> As the Father has life in himself, so he has granted the Son also to have life in himself. And he has given him authority to execute judgment, because he is the Son of Man. (John 5:26–27)

> "My Father is still working, and I also am working." For this reason the Jews were seeking all the more to kill him, because he was not only breaking the Sabbath, but was also calling God his own Father, thereby making himself equal to God. (John 5:17–18 NRSVUE)

I'm not sure what Jesus could have said to make it more clear that he was God. And it won't work to counter that these statements were composed by the church as it tried to deify Jesus, since they were written when eyewitnesses to his earthly life were still living.

C. S. Lewis makes the point better than I can. I sometimes wonder if *Mere Christianity* will be required reading in heaven for those who didn't read it on earth. Consider Lewis's most oftquoted words:

> I am trying here to prevent anyone saying the really foolish thing that people often say about Him: "I'm ready to accept Jesus as a great moral teacher, but I don't accept His claim to be God." That is the one thing we must not say. A man who was merely a man and said the sort of things Jesus said would not be a great moral teacher. He would either be a lunatic—on a level with the man who says he is a poached egg—or else he would be the Devil of Hell. You must make your choice. Either this man was, and is, the Son of God: or else a madman or something worse. You can shut Him up for a fool, you can spit at Him and kill Him as a demon; or you can fall at His feet and call Him Lord and God. But let us not come with any patronizing nonsense about His being a great human teacher. He has not left that open to us. He did not intend to.[55]

Note again that Christians claimed divinity for Jesus during a time when eyewitnesses to his life would quickly have contradicted them if they were wrong. For instance, consider Paul's summary of the Christ event:

> I handed on to you as of first importance what I in turn had received: that Christ died for our sins in accordance with the scriptures and that he was buried and that he was raised on the third day in accordance with the scriptures and that he appeared to Cephas, then to the twelve. Then he appeared to more than five hundred brothers and sisters at one time, most of whom are still alive, though some have died. Then he appeared to James, then to all the apostles. (1 Corinthians 15:3–7 NRSVUE)

Scholars now believe that Paul received this statement from other Christians between three and eight years after Jesus's crucifixion. If Paul received it at such an early date, the creed must have been taught even earlier. For all practical purposes, this statement must have been composed when the original events occurred.[56] In addition, it has been proven that it takes more than two generations, and usually much longer, for an event to become a myth.[57]

Jesus's first followers were completely committed to the truth of his claims to divinity. Consider the implausibility of this claim. The only Son of God, existing before time began, ruling the universe alongside the only God and Father of all creation, chose to enter the world during their lifetime. He was the only baby to choose his parents, and yet he chose a peasant teenager for his mother and a poor Galilean carpenter to be his earthly father. He was the only baby to arrange the circumstances of his birth, and yet he chose a cave behind a crude traveler's inn outside a tiny country town, with only dirt-caked field hands to witness his entrance into the human race.

He then grew up in a village so small it is not named even once in the entire Old Testament. He picked fishermen and tax collectors to be his disciples. He died as a convicted felon on a cross. Then he came back to life and ascended into heaven. It's all too incredible to be imagined.

And yet Peter and the other apostles refused to stop preaching these very claims, even when their lives were threatened (Acts 5:27–32). While there were at least fifty tombs of holy men that became sites of religious veneration during the time of Jesus, there is no evidence that Christians ever venerated the tomb of their Lord, for one simple reason: It was empty.[58] Each one of the apostles except for John was martyred for serving this Lord; John was exiled to the prison island of Patmos for preaching about him. Billions of people across twenty centuries have accepted the claims of these first Christians and followed their Lord as the God of the universe.

How Do We Know He Was Right?

So Jesus claimed to be God, and his early followers believed him. But Muslims believe the testimony of Mohammed and Buddhists believe the teachings of Buddha. Is there objective evidence that Christians are right about Christ?

Here is the rope from which Christianity swings, the one fact that makes or breaks our faith:

> If there is no resurrection of the dead, then Christ has not been raised, and if Christ has not been raised, then our proclamation is in vain and your faith is in vain. We are even found to be misrepresenting God, because we testified of God that he raised Christ—whom he did not raise if it is true that the dead are not raised. (1 Corinthians 15:13–15 NRSVUE)

We have seen the proof that Jesus existed and was crucified at the hands of Pontius Pilate. We know that the first Christians believed him to be raised from the dead. Before Easter, the disciples were sure that their leader was dead and gone. After that day they were transfused with divine courage and set out to win the world for Jesus. But believing doesn't make it true.

David Hume, known today as the father of skepticism, was an eighteenth-century Scottish philosopher who made it his life's work to debunk assumptions that he considered to be unprovable. For Hume, among the unprovables was belief in miracles. He suggested six criteria to judge those who claim to have witnessed a miracle. These miracle reporters should be:

- numerous
- intelligent
- educated
- of unquestioned integrity
- willing to undergo severe loss if proven wrong
- making claims that are capable of easy validation.[59]

These criteria are an excellent tool for measuring the truthfulness of a witness. How do the eyewitnesses to the risen Christ fare by this list?

These witnesses were *numerous*: Over five hundred saw the resurrected Lord (1 Corinthians 15:6). They were *intelligent* and *well educated*—the books they wrote make that clear.[60] Paul was in fact trained by Gamaliel, the finest scholar of Judaism (Acts 22:3). The Christ followers were men and women of *unquestioned integrity*, clearly *willing to undergo severe loss*, as proven by their martyrdoms. And their claims were *easily validated*, as witnessed by the empty tomb anyone could view—"this was not done in a corner" (Acts 26:26 NRSVUE).

So the witnesses were credible. But is there objective evidence for their claims? It is a fact of history that Jesus of Nazareth was crucified and buried, and that on the third day his tomb was found empty. Skeptics have struggled to explain his empty tomb ever since.

Three of their ideas point to theft. The first one claims that Jesus's disciples stole his body while the guards at the tomb slept (Matthew 28:11–15). But how would sleeping guards know the identity of these thieves? How could the disciples convince five hundred people that the corpse was alive? And why would these disciples then die for what they knew to be a lie?

A second approach claims that the women stole the body. But how would they overpower the guards? How would they make a corpse look alive? Why would they suffer and die for such a fabrication?

A third explanation is that the authorities stole the body. When the misguided disciples found an empty tomb, they mistakenly announced a risen Lord. But why would the authorities steal the body they had stationed guards to watch? When Christians began preaching the resurrection, wouldn't they quickly produce the corpse to discredit them?

A fourth approach is the wrong tomb theory: The grief-stricken women and apostles went to the wrong tomb, found it empty, and began announcing the miracle of Easter. But in fact, the women saw where Jesus was buried (Matthew 27:59–61); Joseph of Arimathea, the owner of the tomb, would have corrected the error (Matthew 27:57–61); and the authorities would have gone to the correct tomb and produced the corpse.

Finally, there is the swoon theory: Jesus did not actually die on the cross. He or his followers bribed the medical examiner to pronounce him dead, then he revived in the tomb, thus appearing to be resurrected. But how could he have survived being wrapped in burial clothes that would have smothered him? In his emaciated condition, how could he have shoved aside the stone and overpowered the Roman guards? How could he have appeared through walls (John 20:19, 26) and then ascended to heaven (Acts 1:9)?

There is only one reasonable explanation for the empty tomb, the changed lives of the disciples, and the overnight explosion of the Christian movement upon the world stage: Jesus Christ rose from the dead. He is therefore the person he claimed to be: our Lord and God. He was justified in making the most stupendous claim in human history, one repeated by no other individual in all of recorded history: "All authority in heaven and on earth has been given to me" (Matthew 28:18).

So Is Jesus God?

You've now surveyed the basic arguments for the divinity of Jesus, looking both at nonbiblical and biblical evidence. You have seen proof in writings other than the Bible that Jesus existed and that the first Christians worshipped him as their risen Lord. You have considered the improbability that the earliest believers would have risked everything for a message they knew to be a lie. You have looked at every possible explanation for the empty tomb.

Yet don't you wish there was more? If Jesus of Nazareth was really the Son of God in the flesh, wouldn't you assume that the entire world would know it? Wouldn't you expect absolute proof that God visited our planet?

I both understand and share those sentiments. But as we noticed in wrestling with the existence of God, we need to step back and ask what more we could ask God to do than what he has done. He sent his Son to join the human race through a virgin birth, announcing the miraculous event with an angelic chorus. That Son lived a perfect, sinless life. He performed miracles never before seen in human history. He was crucified in full public view, buried in a guarded grave, and raised from the dead on the third day. His critics have never been able to explain his empty tomb. He appeared alive to more than five hundred people, then ascended to heaven in full view of more than a hundred. He gave us the New Testament, written by chosen people inspired by his Holy Spirit to transmit this information to the world—a text preserved over two thousand years with remarkable and trustworthy accuracy.

Suppose God did it all again in our lifetime so we wouldn't have to depend on ancient records and evidence. Would our response be any different from the responses of his first eyewitnesses? Some believed that his miracles and resurrection were real, but others did not. Jesus could suddenly appear at your side as you read this book, but you might decide that your senses are deceiving you. If you don't believe that miracles are possible, no miracle can convince you otherwise. And in a world where AI makes it increasingly difficult to separate what's true from what's made up, it's difficult to believe we would fare any better than those who heard and saw Jesus two thousand years ago.

I remember visiting two of my relatives as a child—Aunt Daisy and Aunt Clara from Buffalo, Missouri. These sisters must have been the reason Missouri is called the "Show-Me State." The world has never seen more-hardened skeptics. Aunt Daisy and Aunt Clara were certain that the government was not to be trusted, that television news was fabricated, and that everything printed in newspapers was made up. If they didn't see it, they didn't believe it.

They were especially dubious about televised reports that men had landed on the moon. They told everyone who would listen that NASA staged the whole thing on some sand dunes in Arizona and kept the money. I remember asking them about the moon rocks I'd seen in a museum. "How do you know they're really from the moon?" they countered. It was a good question.

My aunts grew up in a day when space flights were the stuff of comic-book fantasy. Everyone knew that it was impossible to go into space, so there was absolutely no evidence on television or in the papers that could convince my aunts that men had actually walked on the moon. I suppose the only way they could have been persuaded would have been to fly to the moon themselves. If any eighty-year-old women could have made the trip, it would have been Aunt Daisy and Aunt Clara.

That's how it is with faith in Jesus. No reporters—biblical or contemporary—can prove his divinity beyond any doubt. But when your physical life ends, you will be absolutely, 100 percent certain about the divinity of Jesus Christ. Before that time comes, you and I will have to take it on faith.

To believe in Jesus's divinity is a faith commitment. Not to believe in his divinity is a faith commitment. I am convinced that the evidence strongly endorses the former. And I can tell you that my personal relationship with Jesus Christ proves to me that he is risen and alive. But the only way you can be sure is to meet him for yourself.

The Son of God would like nothing better.

For Further Reflection

- Do you think that non-Christian evidence for Jesus would be persuasive for a skeptic? Why or why not?
- In defending the deity of Christ, how would early Christian evidence for Jesus strengthen or weaken the argument?
- Critics sometimes argue that Jesus never claimed to be God. What is your response?
- How would a skeptic respond to evidence regarding the historicity of the resurrection? How would you answer this objection?

CHAPTER 5

Is Jesus the Only Way to God?

Is faith in Jesus the only way to get to heaven? You might agree that God exists, the Bible is trustworthy, Christianity is a good moral choice, and Jesus is divine. But is he the only way to God?

Muslims, Buddhists, Hindus, and Jews certainly don't think so. I might tell you that over two billion Christians can't be wrong, but that would mean that almost six billion people are. What are we to say to them?

I was twenty-one years old when I first had to face that question. When I was chosen to go to East Malaysia as a summer missionary in 1979, I had never been overseas. I had never met a Buddhist or a Muslim. I knew virtually nothing of what other religions taught. I guess I somehow assumed that Christians were the only people who really believed in God, and that was that.

Imagine my shock when I watched Muslims come out of their mosques after evening prayer, some with their foreheads bleeding from the fervency with which they had bowed on their prayer rugs. Consider my confusion when I watched Buddhists build an altar with paper money on the grave of an ancestor, then burn it so it could be spent in the afterlife. Envision my look of surprise when I encountered Buddhist prayer altars or venerated copies of the Qur'an in every home I entered. *What makes us right and everyone else wrong?* I wondered.

If you've read the first four chapters of this book, you know why I believe that Jesus is Lord. But it is conventional wisdom today to claim that my beliefs are just that—my beliefs. What about the person who says, "Jesus may be your God, but that doesn't make him mine"? Intolerance is the unpardonable sin of our culture. None of us want to seem judgmental or narrow-minded. We can believe that Jesus is God, but why should everyone else have to agree with us? If there's no such thing as objective truth, how can "Jesus is Lord" be objectively true?

This is the problem called postmodernism. It may be the greatest challenge to objective biblical Christianity today. Let's learn where it came from, and how to respond.

Biblical Truth Becomes Church Dogma

The first Christians were absolutely sure about biblical authority. The apostle Peter's Pentecost sermon quoted passage after passage from the Old Testament. Before he was martyred for his faith, Stephen's defense in Acts 7 was largely a retelling of the biblical history of Israel. James led the Jerusalem Council to accept gentiles, arguing from the Old Testament Prophets

(Acts 15). Paul could state with assurance that "all scripture is inspired by God" (2 Timothy 3:16 NRSVUE).

Soon, however, Christian leaders began to insist that the church possesses the only authority to interpret the Scriptures. Since God gave the Bible through the church, he leads the church to show us how to understand it. Ignatius, bishop of Antioch, believed that the bishop should be seen as the authority of a local congregation, and a college of bishops as the ruling authority of the universal church. Irenaeus further identified the church at Rome as the *preeminent authority* in Christendom, and taught that her authority comes from Peter and Paul through the bishops who succeeded them.

Before long (ca. AD 250), Cyprian of Carthage separated the clergy from the laity and made his famous claim, "He can no longer have God for his Father, who has not the Church for his mother."[61] When Constantine converted to Christianity in AD 312 and legalized the church, the authority of the Christian movement was clearly defined as the Church in Rome.

This view of authority greatly molded the church's understanding of biblical authority. Creeds, councils, and papal rulings became the means by which the Scriptures were understood and transmitted.

Protestant reformers sought to relocate authority with the Bible as it is interpreted by the individual believer. When Martin Luther was on trial at the Diet of Worms for his works that challenged the equality of the pope and Catholic Church writings with the teachings of Scripture, he argued that the Bible alone bore the weight of final authority. He concluded his defense by stating simply, "Here I stand. I cannot do otherwise. God help me. Amen."[62] John Calvin agreed, claiming that "God bestows the actual knowledge of himself upon us only in the Scriptures."[63] He went on to write that "the authority of Scripture derived not from men, but from the Spirit of God," and that arguing otherwise is "insulting to the Holy Spirit."[64]

From then to now, Christians have held two views of spiritual authority: the Bible as interpreted by the church (the Catholic position), and the Bible as interpreted by believers (the Protestant position). Catholics disagreed with the way Protestants sought the truth of God, and Protestants returned the favor. But neither group of Christians thought to question the existence of truth itself.

The Truth Becomes *My* Truth

What came next would change Western culture dramatically and create the society you and I live in today. I'll try to tell the story as briefly as possible.

Imagine a debate with three opponents. On the left stands René Descartes (1596–1650), a Catholic mathematician who wanted to defend rationally his church's authoritarian system. He discovered that he could doubt everything except the fact that he was doubting and thus thinking. "I think, therefore I am" became his motto. Truth is known through the use of reason. But how do the senses relate to the mind?

Behind the lectern on the right stands David Hume (1711–1776), the father of skepticism we met in the last chapter. Hume claims that we know nothing except what our senses tell us. Empiricism is the only way to knowledge. But again, what is the relation of the senses to the mind?

Immanuel Kant (1724–1804) then steps to the middle podium with his solution: Our minds interpret what our senses say, resulting in knowledge. Your senses are the keyboard, your mind the software; the resulting knowledge goes on the hard drive and the printer paper.

This is how nearly everyone in the Western world has viewed the world since Kant. According to him, we cannot know reality—only our experience of it. We can know only what our senses tell our minds. If your senses say that this book's paper is white and mine say that it is beige, we'll have to agree to disagree. (If we're Americans, we'll take a vote.)

Apply this idea to Christian faith, and the Bible becomes a diary of religious experiences. My sermon last Sunday is just my truth. Your ideas about God are just your ideas. If Kant is right, the best we can do is to be sincere in our beliefs and tolerant of the beliefs of others. Truth is what works for us. In the world of my parents and grandparents, if an idea was right it must be relevant. Today, if an idea is relevant, it might be right.

A Truthful Response

If you can't get past this objection, you'll have no reason to care about the topics that follow this chapter. There would be no reason to wonder about people who never hear the gospel, or those who struggle with the problem of suffering, question divine sovereignty and human freedom, or wonder what prayer is really for. If all I can give you is my truth, and my opinions are no more valuable than anyone else's (which they're not), I can stop writing and you can stop reading.

But I'm not going to stop writing, for the following reasons. First, consider a logical response. "There is no such thing as absolute truth," we're told. Is this statement absolutely true? If it's not, we can disregard it. If it is, it isn't. This is a paradox, something like the statement "I am lying right now." If that's true, then I just lied, which means that I just told the truth. But if I told the truth, I told a lie. And so on and so on in an endless circle.

The claim that there is no objective truth is an objective truth claim. This is not a new thought. The Skeptics, a Greek philosophical school that was popular three centuries before Christ, had the same idea: "There's no such thing as truth, and we're sure of it." See the problem?

Second, there's an ethical response. If all ethics are purely pragmatic and subjective, no ethical position can be rejected on its merits. How should we view such tragedies as the Holocaust and 9/11? Within the Third Reich, Auschwitz and Dachau were seen as necessary means to a defensible end. And yet they stand as the quintessential rejection of the tolerance so valued by postmodern thinkers. When the bomb-carrying terrorists of 9/11 attacked, they absolutely believed that they were serving the cause of their faith and God. When such immoral acts are committed by people who are convinced they're right, postmodern people must choose between inclusion and intolerance. They cannot have it both ways.

Third, there's a pragmatic response if our postmodern friends simply shrug their shoulders and say, "So what?" Their rejection of objective, scientific truth actually can work in our favor. There was a day when skeptics insisted on empirical proof and scientific verification of the claims of Christianity. While such skepticism still exists, today's postmodern person insists that all claims to truth are equally (though relatively) valid. This thinking has resulted in an interest in spirituality unprecedented in the last hundred years. While this interest unfortunately embraces all alternatives, at least Christianity can be one of the options.

How can we communicate the gospel in such a marketplace of spiritual competitors? By reversing the modern strategy. In the mid-twentieth century we told our culture, "Christianity is true; it is therefore relevant and attractive." We invited nonbelievers to accept the Christian faith on the basis of its biblical, objective merits. "The Bible says" was the only authority Billy Graham's sermons required.

In this postmodern culture we must use exactly the opposite strategy. Today our faith must be attractive, then it may be relevant, then it might be true (at least for its followers). If we can show postmodern seekers of spiritual meaning that Christianity is attractive, interesting, and appealing, they may be willing to explore its relevance for their lives. When they see its relevance for Christians, they may decide to try it for themselves. And when it works, they will decide that it is true for them. Then they will affirm the authority of the Bible and the truthfulness of the Christian faith, not in order to come to faith but because they already have.

Can such an approach be effective? If we appeal to our culture on the basis of attractive relevance, will we abandon our biblical heritage? Actually, we'll return to it.

We live in a postmodern, postdenominational, post-Christian culture. The first Christians lived in a premodern, predenominational, pre-Christian world. They had no hope of taking the gospel to the ends of the earth by appealing to the Roman world on the basis of biblical authority. The Greco-Roman culture shared the postmodern skepticism of any absolute truth claim, let alone those made on the basis of Hebrew Scriptures or a Jewish carpenter's teachings. So the early Christians had to build their evangelistic efforts on personal relevance and practical ministry. The result was the beginning of the most powerful, popular, and far-reaching religious movement in history.

I am convinced that we are now living in a culture more like that of the first Christians than any we have seen since their day. They had no buildings or institutions where they could gather together and engage a skeptical world, so they went *to* that world with the gospel. They had no objective authority base from which to work, so they demonstrated the authority of the Scriptures by proving their attractive, personal relevance. We now live in a day when nonbelievers seldom come to our buildings to listen to our appeals on the basis of biblical authority. But when we show them the practical value of biblical truth in our lives, ministries, and communities, we will gain a hearing.

For instance, many college students and young adults are passionately concerned about the environment and global warming. We can show them that God was the first environmentalist, creating our planet and calling us to care for it. Then we can put our theology into practice by leading our churches and members to be as environmentally conscious as possible.

Racial injustice is a passionate cause for many young people, as it should be for all of us. When churches take the lead in advancing civil rights and cultural understanding, we prove that God's universal love is real in us. Pro-life advocates gain a greater hearing when we become involved in the lives of women struggling with an abortion choice and offer unconditional grace to their families.

When we tell our personal stories of spiritual transformation, we show a postmodern world that Christianity works, because it works in us. My friend Ken Medema sings, "Don't tell me I have a friend in Jesus until you show me I have a friend in you." When we love our neighbors as ourselves, we earn the right to ask our neighbors to love our God.

Every postmodern person I have met wants the same thing: a faith that is practical, loving, and hopeful. The tragedy is that our churches do not always offer them this biblical truth in a way that is attractive and relevant. The good news is that we can.

What About Other Ways to God?

We have considered the evidence that documents the resurrection and thus the divinity of Jesus Christ. We have seen that truth is objective, whether we believe it to be so or not. We have learned that if Christians will show that Jesus is alive through their character and service, many skeptics will consider the relevance of Christianity for their lives as well.

But what about the person who concedes that Jesus is the Son of God and a way to God, but still wonders if he is *the only way* to God? I suppose it is plausible to think that he is risen and thus divine, and that we can be transformed when we come to God by him, but that he is not the only means of such transformation. You can follow my directions and get to my house for dinner, but that doesn't mean that they are the only way to get there. Just because Christians are right doesn't necessarily mean that all other religions are wrong, does it?

What Does the Bible Say?

Several facts are clear in God's Word and essential to our question. First, *Jesus alone claimed divinity*. In John 14:9 he asserted, "Whoever has seen me has seen the Father." Earlier the authorities tried to stone him to death specifically because he claimed to be God (John 10:33).

Other religious leaders have claimed to reveal God; Jesus alone claims to *be* God. It would be blasphemy for a Muslim to say that Muhammad was God. The Buddha never claimed to be God and in fact taught that there is no personal God. No one in Hindu or Jewish history ever claimed to be God. But Jesus did.

Second, *Jesus is preparing our place in heaven* (John 14:2). Other religious leaders taught about heaven or the afterlife; Jesus alone claims to be preparing it for us. No other leader or prophet in the history of world religions ever made such a claim.

Third, *Jesus will take us to heaven personally* (John 14:3). Other religious leaders taught about the way to heaven; Jesus alone claims to take us there.

Fourth, *Jesus is the only way to the Father* (John 14:6). His Greek was emphatic: "I am *the* way, and *the* truth, and *the* life" (emphasis mine). Later he was even more emphatic: "All authority in heaven and on earth has been given to me" (Matthew 28:18). No one in all of human history ever made this claim. Peter would later make the same claim about Christ (Acts 4:12).

Muhammad claimed to have recorded the revelation of Allah and the way to heaven, but he never claimed to be that way. Buddha claimed to teach the way to enlightenment, but he was not the way. Hindu masters claim to teach the way to oneness with Brahman (reality), but none claim to be the way. Jewish rabbis claim to teach the Torah, the law of God and way to eternal life with him, but none claim to have inspired the Law or be the way to God. Only Jesus made such a staggering claim about himself.

We may agree or disagree with him, but we need to know what he believed about himself. He never claimed to be a religious teacher or leader, or one way to God among many. He claimed to be the only way to eternity in heaven.

What Do Other Religions Offer?

It is commonplace today to claim that the world's religions are different roads up the same mountain, different faiths in the same God. Such a claim is astonishing to those who actually follow the various faith traditions. They know that if one is right, the others are by definition and necessity wrong.

Let's begin with Islam. Muslims consider the Qur'an to be the revelation of Allah (the Arabic name for *God*) to mankind, given in the Arabic language. Muslims recognize five primary ways of serving Allah and gaining eternity with him (the Five Pillars of Islam):

- State with full conviction the central claim of Islam: "I bear witness that there is no God but God, and that Muhammad is his prophet."
- Pray five times each day while facing the Holy City of Mecca.
- Give alms (2.5 percent of one's income and net worth) to the poor.
- Fast, especially during the holy month of Ramadan.
- Make a pilgrimage to Mecca at least once. If you are unable, provide for another to go in your place.

A sixth pillar is recognized by some Muslims: death during a declared holy war (a jihad). Muslims believe that we will live individually and consciously for all eternity, either in heaven or in hell.

Hinduism, one of the oldest religions in the world, centers on a similar kind of works righteousness. Its famous doctrine of karma is illustrated by this statement in one of Hinduism's sacred writings: "According as one acts, according as one conducts himself, so does he become. The doer of good becomes good. The doer of evil becomes evil. One becomes virtuous by virtuous action, bad by bad action."[65]

Hindus believe that reality (Brahman) is the One who is the "source of all." Humans are *atman*, a part of Brahman. Atmans are immortal: "nobody can kill the atman; the verb 'to kill' means nothing but 'to separate the atman from the body.' The atman . . . is not born when the body is born and does not die when the body dies, whether in individual life or in cosmic life."[66]

Yoga in the context of Hindu religious practice is the spiritual discipline required to reach the atman's identification with Brahman. Karma-yoga is centered on selfless good works, jnana-yoga stresses the path to oneness through contemplation and knowledge, and bhakti yoga emphasizes emotion or devotion. Hindus believe that we will ultimately achieve *moksha* (salvation), where we are absorbed into Brahman and cease to exist individually.

Buddhists believe that all suffering is due to desire, and that the renunciation of wrong desires leads to *nirvana*, or enlightenment. They follow the Four Noble Truths: Life is suffering, the origin of suffering is wrong desire, the cessation of wrong desire leads to the cessation of suffering, and the cessation of wrong desire comes from living by the Noble Eightfold Path (right view, thought, speech, action, livelihood, effort, mindfulness, and concentration). Like Hindus, Buddhists believe that we will one day become part of reality and cease to exist as individuals.

Judaism is practiced today in three main traditions. The Orthodox are the most committed to living by a literal interpretation of Torah, the Conservative are less literalistic than the Orthodox, and the Reformed are the most liberal (so much so that many among the Orthodox do not consider them true members of the faith). However, each of these traditions focuses in its own way on obedience to the law as the means of pleasing God and receiving his mercy in eternity.

As you can see, these are very different views of eternity and salvation. If Hindus and Buddhists are right about eternity, Muslims, Jews, and Christians must be wrong. If we achieve heaven through the Five Pillars of Islam, all other religions are wrong about salvation. Only Christianity offers eternal life by God's grace through faith, apart from human works (Ephesians 2:8–9). These are not different roads up the same mountain, but very different mountains.

Who Is Right?

There are several ways in which Christian theologians defend the superiority of their faith. One is to consider the miraculous origin of the Christian movement. Christianity clearly stands on the factual, historical miracle of the resurrection. However, Muslims consider the inspiration and reception of the Qur'an to be miraculous; Hindus and Buddhists point to the supernatural nature of moksha or nirvana; and Jews remind us of their miraculous Exodus and the revelation of God in the Old Testament.

I doubt that followers of other faiths will concede that our faith alone can claim supernatural origin. Christians counter that the evidence for the resurrection is remarkably persuasive, but defenders of other faiths will claim the same for their founding events.

A second approach is to examine the evidence for each world religion. What proof can Muslims offer that the Qur'an was truly given by God to the illiterate Muhammad? What evidence can Buddhists offer for the enlightenment of their founder? How do Hindus really know that reincarnation is true and that moksha is possible? By contrast, we have examined remarkable evidence for the trustworthiness and authority of the Bible and for the resurrection and divinity of Jesus.

However, as I have spoken across the years with numerous followers of other faiths, I have not found this argument to be compelling for them. Every Muslim I have ever met was convinced that the Qur'an is the trustworthy revelation of God. And Hindus and Buddhists seldom seek empirical evidence for a personal, supernatural experience. It is hard for us as Christians to prove the uniqueness of our conversions to people who are just as convinced about the merits of their own religious experiences.

A third response is to point to the millions of lives changed by the gospel in the decades following the birth of the church. It is an astounding fact that so many people quickly accepted the apostles' message about a crucified carpenter, and that their movement would survive and grow long after the world's mightiest empire had fallen.

At the same time, other religions have their legions of followers as well. Islam is the fastest-growing religion in the world. Millions of Buddhists and Hindus claim that their religion has transformed their lives. Jews have held to their religious convictions despite horrific persecution. If I claim that Jesus changed my life but you claim that the Qur'an did the same for you, we are at an impasse.

The bottom line is that I'm not sure Christians can prove to non-Christians that our faith is right and all others are wrong. We can remove the roadblocks to Christian faith that would be created if the Bible were untrustworthy or Jesus was no different from any other religious leader. By communicating the facts regarding biblical authority and Jesus's divinity, we can show the reasonable and evidential nature of our faith.

In addition, we can point to the unique nature of the Christian movement. Unlike other religions, Christianity was founded by a person who claimed to be divine. Unlike other religious founders, Jesus rose from the dead. Unlike other religious movements, early Christians came to Christ despite horrendous opposition (and still continue to grow most quickly where they are persecuted most fiercely). Unlike other religious teachings, Christianity offers the absolute assurance of salvation by God's grace, received by personal faith.

I admit that these facts are not so logically conclusive that they prove the truth of Christianity and the falsehood of all other faiths. Like all empirical and rational evidence, they can encourage our personal commitment but they cannot compel it. As we have seen repeatedly, faith in Christ is like all other personal relationships—it requires a commitment transcending the evidence.

How does the Bible tell us to demonstrate the truthfulness of Christianity? Not so much by our logic as by our love. We are called to love our Lord and our neighbor (Matthew

22:34–40). We are promised that everyone will know that we follow Jesus when they see his love in our lives (John 13:35).

Once we testify to the truth we believe and demonstrate God's love in our lives, we can trust the salvation of others to the Holy Spirit. Human words cannot change human hearts. Only the Spirit can convict us of our sins and need for salvation. Only he can make Jesus real to those who want him.

This fact was very good news when I first understood it. Like many Christians, I was nervous in sharing my faith with others. It felt as if I was on trial and the person I was trying to win to Christ was the prosecuting attorney looking for flaws in my argument. Then I came across a different courtroom analogy for the witnessing experience.

When Christians share their faith, Jesus is the one on trial. The person deciding for or against him is the jury. Satan is the prosecuting attorney; the Holy Spirit is the defense attorney. We are witnesses called to the stand. As with all courtroom witnesses, it is our responsibility simply to tell what we know when we are asked to tell it. But the verdict is not up to us.

We may be the first witness called to the stand, or the last. We may never hear the verdict—especially the joy of being in the courtroom when the jury decides in favor of Jesus. But the outcome of the case does not depend on us. We cannot convince anyone that Jesus is Lord. That is the work of the Holy Spirit.

In the meantime, it is our privilege to tell the world about the only way that leads to God. It doesn't bother me that only one key in my pocket will start my car, so long as that key works. Years ago, when my mother was diagnosed with cancer, our family was not upset that Mom didn't have twenty different chemotherapy regimens to choose from—we were grateful for the one that cured her cancer and saved her life. I'm not frustrated that only one road leads to the front door of my house so long as it takes me home.

Only Christianity works where we need God's help the most. Our basic problem with God is called sin. We have all made mistakes and committed sins in our lives. These failures have separated us from a pure and holy God. The only way to heaven that works is the way that deals with these sins. And only Christianity does that. No other religion offers forgiveness for sins, grace for sinners, and the security of salvation. Only Jesus saves.

Is Jesus the Only Way to God?

This chapter, like those before it, was written to lay the groundwork for the questions to come in the next chapters. We will soon begin to explore issues such as God's foreknowledge and our freedom, evil and suffering, the destiny of the unevangelized, and the logic of prayer. But we cannot have much of a conversation if we do not believe that God exists and that Christianity is true.

When I wonder if the Christian faith can stand up to any challenge and change any life, I think about a twelve-year-old boy I met during my summer mission experience back in 1979. Before my partner and I flew into Malaysia to begin our work there, we went through a week of training with career missionaries in Singapore. One evening, as I was talking with two of these missionaries, a young boy happened to walk by and one missionary called him over and introduced him to me. The boy shyly shook my hand and ran off to play with his friends. The missionary then told me his story.

This boy had come to faith in Christ during a Bible study that the church conducted in his nearby apartment building. He very quickly became passionate about his Lord. He never missed a worship service on Sunday or Wednesday. He read his Bible and prayed fervently. He became a great witness to others in his community.

Soon the missionaries began to notice bruises and welts on the young boy's body. One day they took his arm, examined the mark, and asked him what had happened. The boy looked sheepishly at the ground before answering. "My daddy is not a Christian, and when I come home from church, he beats me for worshipping Jesus."

The missionary was shocked and asked the boy why he continued coming to church. The boy was equally surprised by the question. He said, "But Jesus said in the Bible that we were supposed to go to church." The missionary, mindful of many converts who had been forced from their homes, asked the boy why he stayed with his family. I'll never forget the boy's answer: "My father is not a Christian. If I leave home, he won't hear about Jesus."

That young boy attended worship services, prayed, read the Scriptures, and offered God's love to the world every day. I don't know what happened to him, or even if he's alive today. But I do know that his faith was real.

On my best days, I want to follow Jesus the way that boy followed Jesus. On my worst days, I still know that I should.

For Further Reflection

- Postmodern thinkers deny the existence of absolute truth; critics counter that this is an absolute truth claim. What do you think the postmodern person would say to that?
- According to this chapter, demonstrating Jesus's relevance is a Christian's best response to the postmodern denial of objective truth. Do you agree or disagree?
- How could you demonstrate the practical relevance of Christian faith today?
- What would you say to someone who claims that all religions teach the same truth and lead to the same God?

PART 2

The Hardest Questions Christians Ask

CHAPTER 6

Where Was God When My Father Died?

I still remember the day when my aunt dropped off a dusty cardboard box at my house. It contained pictures and memorabilia she had found in her father's things. My grandfather died at the age of ninety-nine. Going through his possessions was like entering a time warp for me. I found yellowed photos of a trip to California our family made when I was in the seventh grade, faded programs from my high school graduation, tattered mementos of family holidays together. And the clearest pictures of my father I've ever seen.

My father's death may be the defining event of my life. His first heart attack came when I was two years old. I learned much later that his left ventricular wall had been so damaged that it could barely function. We lived in Houston so he could use the world-renowned medical facilities there; he personally knew two giants in cardiovascular surgery—heart surgeons Michael DeBakey and Denton Cooley. There was little they could do for him except regulate his blood thinners, so Dad went in nearly every week for tests. My father lived by force of will for nineteen years. When I was a senior in college, he pushed our clothes dryer out from the wall to unkink the vent hose. His heart burst and he died. It was ten days before Christmas.

I was at my pastor's home at the time, preparing a trumpet arrangement to play with the pastor's wife and son the next day. My brother called to tell me that dad was sick and I needed to come home. Somehow I knew it was more, and I drove across Houston at 80 mph, blinkers flashing. I still remember the orange and blue sunset as the winter evening descended. I walked into the emergency room of the north Houston hospital and asked the nurse where my father was. The look on her face told me everything. She led me to the family waiting room where my mother and brother sat staring at the floor. Tears still come to my eyes as I remember that scene, one of the most vivid in my entire life story.

It's been nearly fifty years, and I've thought about my father nearly every day since. Part of the reason why his death is still unresolved for me is that we had so much closure left to do. He never really came to terms with my decision to go into ministry. He had hoped that I would be a doctor or a lawyer rather than a Baptist preacher. If one of my sons suddenly decided to become a Mormon missionary, I would probably feel the same way my dad did about my choice of vocation.

My father had been a Sunday school teacher in the Methodist church before he left for World War II. After witnessing firsthand the atrocities of war, he seldom went to church after he returned. He could never come to terms with why God allowed such horrible suffering in the world. He didn't live long enough for us to discuss the most important issues of my adult life, questions about marriage and finances and parenting. The great tragedy of my life is that my father never met my sons. I still tear up thinking about the loving grandfather he would have been.

But the even tougher, soul-wrenching reason his death still bothers me is that I don't understand it. He was only fifty-five years old. We had so much life still to live together. He was one of the best men I've ever known. No son was more loved by his father. His heart condition prevented him from playing sports with me, so we spent time fishing and working on cars together. When I was a boy, he would come into my bedroom every night before I went to sleep and we'd talk about my day. He never missed one of my band concerts, and he congratulated me for every good grade or award I ever received. The last time I saw him alive was the day he drove across Houston to give me money for a down payment on Janet's engagement ring. If his heart disease had been the result of wrong choices he had made, I might be able to understand. If he had died of liver disease from drinking or lung disease from smoking, or even if he had been killed in World War II, that would be different. But he did nothing to deserve his heart disease. Nothing to deserve a life so dominated by its restrictions. Nothing to deserve such an early death.

Why did my all-powerful and all-loving God allow him to die? I know that we live in a fallen world where heart disease and AIDS and cancer are consequences of humanity's rebellion against God. I understand that heart disease did not exist in the Garden of Eden. But I also know that God sometimes heals heart disease. He sometimes intervenes in the natural order of things. Why not this time, when I needed his help most?

If God would not heal my father, would he heal my sons if something happened to them? Can I trust God with my wife and our future? Can I trust him with the greatest fears I face today? If I cannot, I'll keep him at arm's length. I'll trust him for my salvation, and I might even serve him with my life. I'll stay away from damaging immorality, and I will do my best to love my family and my work. But I will never completely trust God with my greatest hopes and fears. The less I ask, the less disappointed I'll be if he doesn't answer. The more self-reliant I am, the less frustrated I'll be with God's refusal to help me with my problems.

I suspect that most Christians have unresolved disappointments with God. We see so much innocent suffering around the world. Millions died and billions were impacted by the COVID-19 pandemic. More than a thousand in Israel perished in Hamas's attack on October 7, 2023, while tens of thousands more died in the war that followed. September 11, 2001, was, in many ways, the defining tragedy for a generation of Americans, and in many ways, the war on terror still feels like it has yet to end.

We read the book of Job with verse after verse describing his personal tragedy, and we earnestly hope God doesn't bring such tragedy into our lives. But in the back of our minds we know that if God allowed it to happen once, he might allow it to happen again. We understand Jesus's crucifixion for our sins, but wish things had turned out better for his first disciples. If Paul was beheaded and Peter crucified upside down, what might happen to me and the people I love?

We want to give our hearts and souls to God, trusting him completely and unconditionally with our great hopes and dreams. But we don't want him to disappoint us. It's safer to serve him than to love him—that way the inevitable tragedies and frustrations of life won't be compounded by a crisis of faith. The less we expect of God, the less disappointed we'll be if he doesn't do what we hope. And the more grateful we'll be if he does.

Understanding the Problem

The issue of evil and suffering is one of the hardest problems Christians must face. Nothing keeps us from intimacy with God like this challenge. In theological language, we're dealing with *theodicy* (from two Greek words for God—*theos*, and justice—*dikē*). Theodicy was coined by the philosopher Gottfried Wilhelm Leibniz in 1710. He defined his term as "the question of the compatibility of metaphysical, physical, and moral evil in the present world order with the justice and absolute power of God."[67]

The Bible is quite willing to ask Leibniz's question of its author. Habakkuk complained to the One who allowed the devastation of his people at the hands of the Babylonians:

> Your eyes are too pure to look on evil;
> you cannot tolerate wrong doing.
> Why then do you tolerate the treacherous?
> Why are you silent while the wicked
> swallow up those more righteous than
> themselves?
> (Habakkuk 1:13 NIV)

Jesus cried from the cross, "My God, my God, why have you forsaken me?" (Matthew 27:46).

The medieval theologian Boethius provided the classic expression of our problem: "If God exists, from whence comes evil?"[68] The pessimistic philosopher Arthur Schopenhauer spoke for many discouraged souls: "The shortness of life, so often lamented, may perhaps be the very best thing about it."[69] There's your uplifting devotional thought for the day.

Christians are especially susceptible to this issue because we believe three apparently contradictory facts to be equally true:

- God is all-loving.
- God is all-powerful.
- Evil exists.

As the Stoic philosopher Epicurus observed, there are four solutions to this dilemma:

- God wants to remove evil but is unable.
- God is able but unwilling.
- God is both able and willing.
- God is neither able nor willing.

We're engaged in combat over the third approach. Can we defend it with intellectual honesty? If so, how?

Victories That Aren't Victories

The easiest way to solve the problem of evil and suffering is to choose one of the other three solutions. For instance, we can decide that God is able to remove evil but is unwilling. In other words, he is not the all-loving God of Christian doctrine. The ancient Stoics were sure that everything is fated by him. They claimed that we are all dogs tied to carts. We can trot alongside the cart or be dragged by it, but we're going with the cart.

The ancient Greeks viewed their gods as capricious and immoral—Zeus throwing lightning bolts at anyone who displeased him. A common secular viewpoint today is that life is random coincidence, and that if there is a God, he has little interest in us. He is a clockmaker who sits dispassionately in heaven and watches his creation slowly wind down.

Or we can decide that God is willing but unable to remove suffering and that, in fact, he is not all-powerful. Religious dualism argues that evil is coequal with good. From ancient Zoroastrianism to today, it has been popular to see God and Satan, good and evil, locked in a battle for supremacy. J. S. Mill asserted that God is limited in his power. He loves us, but cannot do everything he would wish to do to help us. Rabbi Harold Kushner, in his kind and sympathetic bestseller *When Bad Things Happen to Good People*, agrees that even God is not able to do everything he wants to do.

A third approach is to minimize the nature or existence of evil. One example is the Hindu belief that evil is *maya*, or illusion. The ancient Greeks saw evil as the product of the material world, something to escape from using rigorous ascetic discipline and philosophical reflection. The Buddhist worldview treats evil as the product of wrong desires. If evil is not real, our problems are resolved.

One other solution is to deny the existence of God altogether. David Hume, the eighteenth-century skeptic, proposed this syllogism:

- If God exists, he must be loving and powerful and thus eradicate evil.
- Evil exists.
- Therefore God does not exist.

While atheism says there is no God, *agnosticism* (from the Greek *gnosis*, or knowledge, and *a*, or no) asserts that we cannot know if he exists or not, or at least that the agnostic cannot. The existence of evil and suffering has probably motivated more people to question or even reject the existence of God than any other factor. I count myself among them.

Approaches That Help

Since theodicy is a problem as old as the Garden of Eden and the Flood of Noah's time, Christian theologians have wrestled with it all through the history of our faith. Five basic approaches have most often been proposed. Each of them gives us much needed help for the battle we're fighting.

Satan Causes Much Suffering

Satan is very real. He murders and lies (John 8:44). He accuses the people of God (Job 1:9–11; Zechariah 3:1), resists the godly (Matthew 13:38–39), and tempts us to sin (1 Chronicles 21:1; Matthew 4:1). He has power over unbelievers (Acts 26:18; 2 Corinthians 4:3–4). He is a "roaring lion looking for someone to devour" (1 Peter 5:8 NIV).

As a result, much of the evil and suffering in the world comes from his malignant work. The apostle Paul was clear: "Our struggle is not against flesh and blood, but against the rulers, against the authorities, against the powers of this dark world and against the spiritual forces of evil in the heavenly realms" (Ephesians 6:12 NIV).

However, not all suffering is the direct result of Satan's handiwork. We live in a fallen world where natural disasters and disease are inevitable. People misuse their free will (see the second approach below). God also permits some suffering for our greater good (see the third approach). Satan would like us to attribute all evil to him, giving him more power in our lives than he would otherwise possess, or blame nothing on him, pretending he doesn't exist.

The right approach is to ask the Lord if there is a Satanic component to our suffering, and know that our Father will guide us to the truth. If we are under attack, we can claim the power of God over our enemy and find victory in his Spirit and strength. When we are tempted, we can pray to our Father and find his help and strength to resist that temptation. When we struggle spiritually, we can turn to his Word and Spirit for power. When we do, we learn once more that "the one who is in you is greater than the one who is in the world" (1 John 4:4 NIV).

We Misuse Our Freedom

Augustine (AD 354–430) is often considered the greatest Christian theologian after Paul. His approach to the problem of evil and suffering can be summarized as follows:

- God created all that is.
- All that he created is good.
- Before the fall, evil was therefore "nonbeing," with the potential to be chosen but not yet reality.
- God created humanity with freedom of will.
- We used this freedom to choose evil.
- Our choice brought evil into existence, absolving God of blame.

There is much in Scripture to commend Augustine's approach. God gave us freedom of will (Genesis 2:15–17; Exodus 32:26; Deuteronomy 30:19; Joshua 24:15; 1 Kings 18:21). We were given this freedom so we could choose God and good (Matthew 4:10; Proverbs 1:10; 4:14; Romans 6:13; Ephesians 6:13; 2 Peter 3:17). Our free choice for wrong led to evil (James 1:13–15; 4:1). All people are now sinners (Romans 3:23). Our sin has resulted in a fallen world (Genesis 3:17; Romans 8:19–22).

Whenever evil is the product of our sinful choices, Augustine's approach explains its existence without blaming God. However, it does not account adequately for innocent suffering. Augustine would argue correctly that hurricanes and tornadoes are the products of a world that fell because of sin. But he could not explain why they would devastate particular cities and neighborhoods rather than some other part of the planet, or why so many innocent children and families would be affected.

A skeptic may also object: If Adam and Eve were completely good when they were created, why would they choose to sin? We might further ask, If God did not create evil, how could the Tree of Knowledge of Good and Evil even exist? And we might wonder, If God gave us freedom of will and knew how we would use it, isn't he responsible to some degree for its use? If I leave rat poison where I know a baby will find it, no court in the land would consider me innocent if the child ate it and died.

The free-will approach helps us understand why a person who chooses to abuse alcohol might die in a drunk driving accident. But it doesn't explain why the innocent driver of the other car had to die as well.

Suffering Builds Character

Irenaeus (ca. AD 120–ca. AD 200) proposed an alternative approach to our problem:

- God created us to develop into a perfect relationship with himself.
- He created the world as a place for that development.
- Evil is thus necessary as a means of our spiritual development (soul-building).

The Bible does teach that some suffering comes from God (Deuteronomy 8:5; Job 16:12; Psalm 66:11; 90:7). We know that suffering can lead to good (Job 23:10; Psalm 119:67; 2 Corinthians 4:17; Hebrews 12:11; Revelation 7:14). Suffering can lead us to repentance (Jeremiah 7:3, 5, 7) and can refine us (Psalm 66:10; Isaiah 48:10; Malachi 3:3; 1 Peter 1:7; 4:17). Pain enables us to witness to our faith in God in spite of the hurt (1 Peter 2:12, 15; 3:15–16). And God promises to use even difficult experiences for our good, in order to make us more like Jesus (Romans 8:28–29).

Irenaeus explained how evil could exist before Adam and Eve chose it.[70] His approach also affirms the hope that God can redeem any suffering for his glory and our good. However, the fall Irenaeus pictured is not as catastrophic as the event described in Genesis 3.[71] And the amount of evil in the world seems disproportionate to the present good. For instance, it is hard to argue that the lessening of anti-Semitism that resulted from the Holocaust justifies the horrors of that tragedy.

This approach also struggles to explain how hell is a place of soul-building. Why would a loving God send people to be punished for all eternity, long after they have learned the reason for their torment and the lessons it might teach?

Present Pain Can Lead to Future Good

Eschatology deals with the future. Applied to theodicy, this approach claims that evil will be resolved in the future, making present suffering endurable and worthwhile. Jesus promised that life on earth leads to life eternal in glory (John 14:1–6), a paradise beyond our imagination (Revelation 21:1–5). The apostle Paul wrote that we should not consider the present sufferings worth comparing with the glory to be revealed (Romans 8:18).

As a philosophical model, this approach offers the guarantee of absolute rational understanding. We do not comprehend the purpose of suffering now, but we will one day (1 Corinthians 13:12). All our questions will be answered. All God's reasons for permitting suffering in our lives will be clarified. Our present faithfulness will be redeemed with future rewards in glory (Revelation 2:10).

However, this approach does not offer much of an explanation in the present. And some might wonder how this promise of future hope makes present courage possible.

God Hurts as We Hurt

The last model is more practical than theoretical: God suffers as we suffer, and he gives us strength to withstand and even redeem our pain. The Bible affirms this assertion (2 Corinthians 4:1, 16; Ephesians 3:13; Hebrews 12:5; Revelation 2:3). God walks with us through the valley of the shadow of death (Psalm 23:4). He weeps as we weep (John 11:35). Jesus experienced every temptation and pain we feel (Hebrews 4:15). He is present with us now in the sufferings of life (Deuteronomy 20:1; Psalm 34:18; Isaiah 43:2; Daniel 3:24–25; Acts 16:25–26).

Philosophically, this approach is not a true theodicy. It offers no real explanation for the origin or existence of suffering. But it does provide the practical assurance that our Father walks with his children through the hardest places of life and will never allow us to face more than he will give us the strength to bear (1 Corinthians 10:13).

Now for the Hard Part

I have taught classes on the problem of evil and suffering since 1984, when I first began teaching philosophy of religion at

Southwestern Baptist Theological Seminary in Fort Worth, Texas. I am grateful for the truth and help these approaches can offer. But whenever I have taught and tried to follow these principles, there has remained an unacknowledged hand in the air at the back of the classroom, a voice of dissent I have tried not to hear: "Yes, but what about innocent suffering? I understand why a drunk driver might be injured in a car crash, but what about the baby killed in the other car? I can see how hard times can build our faith, but does that fact justify atrocities and tragedies like 9/11, October 7, or a global pandemic? I'm sure warning systems for future hurricanes will be more effective, but if they can't stop the hurricane, does that future good make sense of present tragedy? You promise me God's presence in unjustified suffering, but I would rather not suffer at all. Wouldn't you?" The answer is yes.

So what do we do about innocent suffering that has no apparent positive result? Why did my father die so young, through no fault of his own? Why did God allow him to die for no good reason I can see? Why does a good and powerful God allow good people to suffer? This is my most urgent question for God, and the reason for the next chapter.

For Further Reflection

- Have you personally experienced innocent suffering in your life? How has this issue challenged your faith? How has it changed it?
- What are the advantages and disadvantages of attributing some evil and suffering to the work of Satan today?
- In your experience, how is the free-will approach to suffering strong? How is it weak?
- In what ways has suffering strengthened your character?
- Does the fact of God's presence help you with the problem of evil and suffering? In what way?

CHAPTER 7

When Suffering Makes No Sense

In the decades I have been a pastor, I have watched in agonizing grief as parents buried their babies. I have stood by, feeling helpless and frustrated, in the hospital rooms of godly parents as they fought terminal illnesses for the sake of their young families. As I write this paragraph I am thinking of a young man in today's news, a tourist from Texas stabbed in the chest while sitting beside his girlfriend on a New York subway train. The only explanation police can suggest is that the crime might have been a gang initiation ritual. Doctors don't yet know if the young man will survive.[72]

Where was God when that criminal got up from his seat to assault his innocent victim? How can any future or present good justify such a crime? If God did not or could not protect that tourist, will my family be safe when we take our next vacation? As my sons drive to their summer jobs this morning, can I trust them to their Father's care?

Visiting with patients in hospital rooms, I often read to them from Psalm 91:

> If you say, "The LORD is my refuge,"
>   and you make the Most High your dwelling,
> no harm will overtake you,
>   no disaster will come near your tent.
> For he will command his angels concerning you
>   to guard you in all your ways;
> they will lift you up in their hands,
>   so that you will not strike your foot against a stone.
> You will tread on the lion and the cobra;
>   you will trample the great lion and the serpent.
> (Psalm 91:9–13 NIV)

Most of the time the patients I visit survive their surgeries and vindicate the psalm's promise. But sometimes they don't. Harm befalls them; disaster comes near their tent. God's angels don't seem to guard them in all their ways. Each time I read Psalm 91, I hope its promise is kept. But I'm always afraid it won't be.

So it's hard for me to give myself completely to a Father whose promises I cannot always trust, whose protection I cannot always depend upon. I am grateful for my salvation from hell, and I know that living according to God's Word is the best way for me to live my life. It has been my honor to serve him as a pastor and teacher of his truth. But innocent suffering remains a significant roadblock to continued spiritual progress for me. I know he wants a deeper, more intimate, and passionate relationship with me. But it's hard to love someone unconditionally when I do not trust his word and ways completely.

This was my father's issue after witnessing the carnage of World War II. Over the years, I've met many who share his struggle and mine. Unexplained grief and innocent suffering have found them as well. Some drop out of church and the Christian life, but most trudge on, as faithful as they know how to be, all the while wishing they could recapture that joy they knew in Jesus before the pain changed everything. But they are resigned to the belief that they probably can't.

I don't claim that the facts that follow will remove all pain and resolve all doubts. If Jesus could cry from the cross, "My God, my God, why have you forsaken me?" (Matthew 27:46), so can we. If Jesus could weep at the grave of his friend Lazarus (John 11:35), we can weep at the graves of those we love.

But I do hope that these facts help. At the very least, they have helped me make sense of innocent suffering. They have become stepping stones through the swamp, a way forward through the mire of doubt and discouragement. They're holding me up so far. I think they'll hold your weight as well.

We're All in This Together

Innocent suffering has been an extremely common fact of life since the world began. The biblical story of Joseph comes to mind immediately—sold into slavery by his jealous brothers, imprisoned on false charges, separated from his home and family for half a lifetime. His descendants were enslaved and abused by their Egyptian masters for four centuries. Job—his name says it all. God's prophets were rejected and despised, imprisoned and martyred.

A million Christians were slaughtered by the Roman Empire in the years before Constantine. I was in Italy recently, visiting the underground catacombs where as many as 250,000 Christians were buried. However, more Christians were killed for their faith in the twentieth century than in the previous nineteen combined.

To me, one of the most confusing scenes in the book of Revelation is the *fifth seal*:

> When he opened the fifth seal, I saw under the altar the souls of those who had been slain because of the word of God and the testimony they had maintained. They called out in a loud voice, "How long, Sovereign Lord, holy and true, until you judge the inhabitants of the earth and avenge our blood?" Then each of them was given a white robe, and they were told to wait a little longer, until the full number of their fellow servants, their brothers and sisters, were killed just as they had been. (Revelation 6:9–11 NIV)

God knew that other believers would be killed for their faith, and he did nothing to stop it. Christians have been dying for their faith ever since.

But Christians are by no means the only people to face innocent suffering. Every infant's death is an outrage. Every abused child is an unspeakable tragedy. Every person who suffers pain that they did not cause or suffering that they did not deserve is added to the list of people awaiting an explanation. This is not an occasional occurrence, an issue easily pushed to the side. It fills our news feeds every day. And it's in the story of every person I know.

So the problem is neither ignorable nor unusual. I cannot evade it. But neither do I face it alone. There's comfort in knowing that this issue is not unique to me, as though I caused it myself. And there's hope in recognizing that the God of the universe cares what happens to the humanity he has made.

Grief has a way of isolating us. Grieving people dress up for church and tell you they're just fine. As you struggle with your grief, you are left feeling that you're the only person going through such pain. But after a while you give in, dress up just as they did, and tell the same lies. The truth is that you're not alone. In fact, if you're facing innocent suffering, you've joined the largest fraternity on earth.

It's Good That God's Not Fair

While we've all dealt with innocent suffering, few of us are truly innocent or sinless. The baby who dies of sudden infant death syndrome is. The toddler killed by an abusive babysitter is. If God were fair, children would never be mistreated. But few of us are sinless.

There are diseases and disasters we did nothing to cause, of course. I know a brilliant doctor and wonderful mother who died of breast cancer. She did not deserve to die. But honesty compels me to admit that most of the pain in my life doesn't fall into the same category as hers. Most of the frustration and suffering I want to blame on God has at least some roots in my own choices and failings.

I'm still angry about a traffic ticket I was given last year for an illegal turn I don't believe I made. But if I hadn't been running late for a dinner meeting, I would never have made that turn at all. I'm frustrated by the hamstring I pulled playing tennis two days ago. But if I were in better shape, I probably would be on the court today.

I don't mean to blame the innocent for their suffering. But I do mean to suggest that not all suffering is innocent, and that we might be grateful God is not more fair to his children. If he were, every time we lied, we'd be caught. Every time we harbored illicit desires, we'd be exposed. Every time we gossiped, our words would be published. If God were completely fair, we should either contract *no* unearned disease or *every* unearned disease. The next time you watch a car speed by and complain, "Where's a policeman when you need one?" you might remember the last time you were speeding and didn't get caught.

Years ago I prepared a sermon titled *Is God Fair?* I worked all week to develop a message that defended the fairness and righteousness of God. As I was walking to my office that Sunday morning, I happened to pass a good friend who was making copies in the church office for her Sunday school class. She looked at her worship program, saw my sermon title, smiled, and said, "Aren't you glad he's not?" I had ten minutes to completely revise my message for the day. That wasn't fair.

There are undoubtedly times when we seem justified in wishing God were more fair. But there may be more times when we should be glad he's not.

The Fall Produced a Fallen World

Our world does not function as God intended it to. In the Garden of Eden, my father would not have suffered from heart disease. No tsunamis would have devastated coastal life. No hurricanes would have destroyed large parts of North Carolina, Jamaica, or any of the other regions hit by massive storms. Cancer and AIDS would be unknown words. But when humanity fell into sin, creation fell with us. So, "we know that the whole creation has been groaning as in the pains of childbirth right up to the present time" (Romans 8:22 NIV).

My point is simply that much innocent suffering is not God's fault. I don't think he caused my father's heart attacks. He did not initiate Hitler's Holocaust. It is tempting to assume that every time life hurts, God caused the hurt. But it's not true. The Lord sent Noah as a "preacher of righteousness" (2 Peter 2:5 NIV), but mankind would not repent. God wanted his people to take the promised land when they first arrived there, but they refused his call and paid for their disobedience with forty years of wilderness wanderings. The Lord sent his prophets to warn the nation of their immorality and his impending judgment, but they would not listen until Assyria and Babylon proved his holiness.

Jesus wept over Jerusalem's refusal to accept his word and grace (Luke 19:41–44). He does not want any to perish, but all to come to repentance (2 Peter 3:9). Tragically, not everyone comes to repentance. In his sovereign power, God has chosen to limit himself to the freedom he has given us. So his will is not always done.

Much innocent suffering does not come from the hand of God. That fact helps me trust him when I hurt. But it doesn't explain why he doesn't always intervene when the suffering comes. If he ever healed a single person with heart disease, why didn't he heal my father? If he ever prevented a single natural disaster, why didn't he protect North Carolina?

Freedom Requires Consequences

Now we are coming to the heart of my struggle with God. I could understand if he sometimes did not want to intervene when his children were hurting because he was not absolutely loving. No one asks how Hitler could do the things he did . . . just why he did them. Conversely, I could understand if God could not intervene when we were suffering because he was not absolutely powerful. No one asks why my grandmother didn't prevent the Holocaust. Granted, I would have a different and larger problem in seeking to trust such a limited God. But at least I would have logically resolved the problem we're discussing.

Of course, the biblical facts are that God is fully loving and fully powerful. And there are times that seem to prove that this is true. I know a woman who was diagnosed with pancreatic cancer and given three months to live. Twenty years later, she was still cancer free. I know a man whose heart stopped on the operating table, and could not be revived by the doctors. As they were removing the equipment, the man's heart started again. But I also knew a dear saint who died of pancreatic cancer, and another whose heart could not be started after his surgery.

If God has ever intervened in the natural order of things, why didn't he do so for my father? He liberated Peter from Herod's prison (Acts 12); why doesn't he free more Christians from prison and martyrdom today? My father didn't deserve his heart disease any more than an infant deserves to die of SIDS.

But consider this fact: If God intervened every time my misused freedom was about to cause suffering for myself and others, I would not be truly free. There can be no freedom without consequences. My wife and I have been watching our diets lately, cutting down on carbohydrates and sugar. If I go off the rails and order a pepperoni pizza for lunch, but the Lord intervenes and the pizza delivery boy brings a salad with grilled chicken instead, my choice was not really a choice. If fast-food restaurants displayed the same menus but began serving only fat-free yogurt, our freedom would be only apparent. Not to mention distasteful.

If God intervened every time a natural disaster was about to bring innocent suffering, the natural order would no longer exist. The same gravity that enables me to sit in this chair and type on this laptop computer would cause my computer to break if I drop it. Someone observed that the man who jumps from an eighth-story window doesn't break the law of gravity—he illustrates it. God could decide to eliminate gravity so airplanes wouldn't crash, but then they couldn't land. Nature often brings good things at the same time it brings hardship. Baseball fans curse the same rain that the farmer welcomes with joy.

There are consequences to freedom, or we're not free. Since God made us to worship him, and worship requires us to make a choice, he won't remove our ability to choose. He could insulate us from the results of our choices, but that's tantamount to removing our freedom. And that's something he'll never do.

I Don't Know What Is Best

I want God to manage his creation so that it always works out for my good. But to be honest, I seldom know what that good really is.

When I was a high school senior, I sensed that God was calling me into vocational ministry. But my first loves were tennis and playing the trumpet, and I didn't want to give up either one. That year I contracted chicken pox, a childhood disease that made me the butt of jokes from my so-called friends. The virus affected a nerve in my neck and paralyzed the right side of my face. The resulting Bell's palsy took away my ability to play my trumpet. I learned the hard way to trust in the One who is greater than a musical instrument and to follow God's will for my life. The paralysis eventually left and I could play again, but my Father's call never left.

I don't believe that God caused my chicken pox, but I will always be grateful for the way he used it in my life. I have learned that I am no judge at all of what is best for my life. I want the Lord to manipulate the world to my personal good, but I don't know what that good really is.

And I seldom know how my desires and experiences impact the rest of my world. A domino that I can see knocks down many that I can't. If Joseph's brothers hadn't sold him into slavery, he could never have saved their lives and the Israelites as a people. If Pharaoh had not sought the death of all Hebrew baby boys, Moses's mother would not have left him to be adopted by Pharaoh's own daughter. If Nebuchadnezzar had not required that the nation pray to him alone, Daniel would not have demonstrated God's power over a lion.

What if King George had been more lenient toward his subjects in the American colonies? What if President Lincoln had listened to naysayers who doubted the ability of Ulysses Grant? If Mexican dictator Santa Anna had honored the Constitution of 1824 instead of declaring himself the Napoleon of the West and inciting Texans to revolt, I might be writing this chapter in Spanish today. If the Japanese high command had called off Pearl Harbor, half the world might be reading this book in Japanese or German. How different would human history be if Ronald Reagan had listened to critics who said an actor could never be president? Or if Boris Yeltsin had yielded to army forces surrounding Moscow?

It is impossible for me to see the future consequences of present occurrences. What seems a tragedy of unredeemable proportion that may lead to future good is beyond my comprehension. And good on earth cannot compare with good in heaven. I have absolutely no way of knowing how God is using present suffering for spiritual and eternal advance, how a child's tragic death will cause untold numbers to trust him for their eternal salvation, or how an unexplained natural disaster is leading thousands to turn from false gods to the one true God.

But I can believe that "our present sufferings are not worth comparing with the glory that will be revealed in us" (Romans 8:18 NIV). And that the God who sees tomorrow better than I can see today knows what is best for both.

Death Is a Blessing to the Person Who Dies

This section is difficult to write, but working through this concept has helped me as much as anything we'll discuss. Most of the suffering we're considering relates to undeserved death—a baby who doesn't survive birth, a child who is killed in a car crash, a young mother who dies after a debilitating battle with leukemia. Our pain in being separated from loved ones is understandable and nearly unbearable. But it may help to know that the one who dies feels nothing that we are enduring. In fact, it takes only a second or so for those who die in Christ to be glad they did.

Jesus told the thief at his side, "Today you will be with me in paradise" (Luke 23:43). *Paradise* was a Persian word for the walled garden of the king. Not only would the thief receive eternal life, he would spend it with the King himself. Jesus taught us that the moment believers die, the angels carry them to Abraham's side, a metaphor for heaven (Luke 16:22). They will be in a far better place than earth (Philippians 1:23). They are forever and always with Jesus.

Jesus could not have been more straightforward or encouraging: "I am the resurrection and the life. The one who believes in me will live, even though they die; and whoever lives by believing in me will never die" (John 11:25–26 NIV). There will never be a moment when a person who trusts in Jesus ceases to be. When that cancer victim who loves her Lord closes her eyes on earth, she opens them in heaven. When the soldier who trusts in God takes his last breath on the battlefield, he takes his first breath in heaven. In that instant, the believer steps from death into life, from the car into the house.

That's why Paul said, "We would rather be away from the body and at home with the Lord" (2 Corinthians 5:8). Think of a small boy who falls asleep in the backseat of the car. When the family gets home, his father picks him up and carries him into the house. When the child wakes up, he's home. That's exactly what happens to God's children.

Such a state is *gain* (Philippians 1:21), for "blessed are the dead who die in the Lord from now on" (Revelation 14:13). They gain imperishable, glorified, spiritual bodies (1 Corinthians 15:42–44) for they are like Jesus (1 Corinthians 15:49). They know God and each other as they are known (1 Corinthians 13:12). And they will eat of the tree of life and live forever (Revelation 22).

It may help to know that people in heaven whom you love feel none of the separation from us that we feel from them. There is no such thing as time in heaven. As C. S. Lewis pointed out, if we think of time as a line on a page, we must see God as the page. He created time, and he transcends it.

For those loved ones in heaven, it will be only a moment before they see us again. Your child will not spend the decades separated from you that you are spending from her. Your spouse or friend is not waiting to see you in the same way you are waiting to see them. In heaven there is "no more death or mourning or crying or pain, for the old order of things has passed away" (Revelation 21:4 NIV).

So death is life for God's children. God's Word expresses his heart: "Precious in the sight of the LORD is the death of his saints" (Psalm 116:15). We understandably grieve for those we love who are no longer with us. But our grief is not for them.

On his deathbed, the great evangelist Dwight Moody exclaimed, "Earth recedes; Heaven opens before me." His son Will, who thought his father was dreaming, attempted to rouse him. In response, Dwight stated, "No, this is no dream, Will. It is beautiful . . . If this is death, it is sweet. There is no valley here. God is calling me. I must go."[73] For those who make Jesus Lord of their lives, when they die, they don't. Instead, they see God. And they are safely home.

The Deaths of Babies and Children

What about babies and children who die before they have a chance to trust in Jesus?

The great miracle of the incarnation is not that God entered the world he made. As Creator, he had every right to visit his creation. The great miracle was that he came as a baby. Rather than appear among us in his heavenly status, the Lord Jesus chose to become one of us—not as an adult but as a fetus who became a newborn, helpless infant. The hands that held the stars were sheltered in a mother's arms. Christmas tells us what God thinks of children.

King David said of his deceased newborn son, "I shall go to him, but he will not return to me" (2 Samuel 12:23). He believed that his child with Bathsheba was already where he would ultimately go one day, and David trusted him to the God who made him.

When Jesus's disciples asked, "Who, then, is the greatest in the kingdom of heaven?" (Matthew 18:1 NIV), "he called a little child to him, and placed the child among them. And he said: 'Truly I tell you, unless you change and become like little children, you will never enter the kingdom of heaven'" (vv. 2–3 NIV). The greatest in God's kingdom is the one who is most like a child.

When some mothers brought their children to Jesus seeking his blessing (a typical custom when a famous rabbi came through the area), Jesus's disciples rebuked those who brought them (Matthew 19:13). But Jesus said to them: "Let the little children come to me, and do not hinder them, for the kingdom of heaven belongs to such as these" (v. 14 NIV).

It is obvious that "Jesus loves the little children, all the children of the world." Our Creator is also "our Father in heaven" (Matthew 6:9). A child who dies before they are old enough to sin against this Father has never broken this relationship. That child has never fallen into sin and away from God. So that child is with the Lord in his paradise.

God Redeems All He Permits

Earlier I admitted that I cannot see all the ways God is using suffering for good. Sometimes I can find no such redemption in my pain. But the fact that I do not know something makes it no less knowable or real. C. S. Lewis observed that the man who denies the sunrise doesn't harm the sun. God is free to use pain for gain, whether I see his love at work or not.

Now I need to add the fact that he always will. God never wastes a hurt. He can be trusted to redeem all he permits. Romans 8:28 is one of the most misunderstood promises in Scripture. It does *not* claim that all things *are* good, that we should pretend that suffering doesn't hurt. Rather, it claims that "in all things God works for the good of those who love him, who have been called according to his purpose" (NIV). He will use anything he allows for his glory and our good.

In fact, his holiness requires him to do so.

> He is the Rock, his works are perfect,
>   and all his ways are just.
> A faithful God who does no wrong,
>   upright and just is he.
> (Deuteronomy 32:4 NIV)

> Was it not I, the Lord?
>   And there is no God apart from me,
> a righteous God and a Savior;
>   there is none but me.
> (Isaiah 45:21 NIV)

> For the word of the Lord is right and true;
>   he is faithful in all he does.
> The Lord loves righteousness and justice;
>   the earth is full of his unfailing love.
> (Psalm 33:4–5 NIV)

The LORD reigns forever;
he has established his throne for judgment.
He rules the world in righteousness
and judges the peoples with equity.
(Psalm 9:7–8 NIV)

For the LORD is righteous;
he loves justice;
upright men will see his face.
(Psalm 11:7 NIV)

The LORD is righteous in all his ways
and faithful in all he does.
(Psalm 145:17 NIV)

Let not the wise boast of their wisdom
or the strong boast of their strength
or the rich boast of their riches,
but let the one who boasts boast about this:
that they have the understanding to know me,
that I am the LORD, who exercises kindness,
justice and righteousness on earth,
for in these I delight.
(Jeremiah 9:23–24 NIV)

God *must* always do the right thing. Everything he causes must achieve a perfect and holy purpose. And everything he permits must do the same. He will use even our misused freedom for his larger glory and his kingdom's good.

Joseph's brothers thought they had dispensed with him, but God used their rejection to save their family. Pharaoh thought he would destroy the Hebrew people, but God used his rebellion to save them. The religious authorities caused the Romans to arrest Paul, an act that saved him from his Jewish persecutors and led to his ministry in Rome. Satan thought he won the battle when Jesus died, but that was the very moment when he lost the war.

The holy God of the universe is required by his own character to redeem all he permits. You and I may not see such good until we're in glory, but we *will* see it there. We will be permitted to know all the ways God used and blessed our pain and sacrifice, our suffering and loss. We will understand why he allowed our loved ones to die, our families to face such adversity, our ministries to encounter such opposition. He will always transform loss into gain. We may not understand how or why he is using bad for good any more than we see the sun on a cloudy day. But we can see everything else in its light.

So What About Innocent Suffering?

Writing this chapter has been therapeutic for me. It has caused me to admit some of my frustrations with God, to expose them, and to wrestle with God over them. I am leaving the ring a better person for the struggle. I hope you can say the same.

It's true that much suffering is the result of our misused freedom, and sometimes it serves as the means to our obvious good in the present or the future. But even the innocent pain we face does not mean that we cannot trust our Father. We don't understand why he has permitted it, but that's only because we seldom know what is best for our lives and cannot see what God is doing to redeem it today and in eternity.

We can, however, count on the fact that he is going to redeem it. His holiness requires it. We can trust what we do not understand to the One who does. And we can draw closer to him in intimate, trusting faith. Not because such faith means we'll never hurt, but because we need such faith when we do. And because our Father permits only what is best for his children.

Coming to that conclusion helps me want to know and love God more than I do. It gives me the courage to trust him even when I know he may not act in ways I want him to. Even though I may find myself disappointed with him again, I am choosing to love him and depend upon him based on the assurance that his holiness permits him to do only what is best for me and those I love.

All relationships transcend the evidence and are self-validating. I couldn't prove to you that Janet loves me or that I love her. In twenty-seven years of marriage I have certainly disappointed her often. But she knows I love her because she continues to trust that I do. If she chose not to trust me any longer, she could not be close enough to me to know that she could.

So it is with my Father. I am choosing to trust in him so that I can know that I can. I am going to depend upon him to do what is right and best, so that he can. That's not to say that I won't shake my fist at him again in the future. But now I know that he won't shake his fist back at me.

A few years ago I was standing beside a baby girl's hospital crib when her parents were advised to remove her life support. There can be no deeper, darker valley in life. As the grieving father held his little girl's hand, he happened to look out the neonatal intensive care unit's window. At just that moment, a pink balloon floated by the window on its way up into the pale blue sky. That young father heard God's Spirit say that if he could release his baby girl, her Father would take her hand and lead her home. And so he did.

At the graveside service, her parents brought balloons for us to release to the heavens. It was hard for me to let mine go. It would be still. But at least I know what happens when I do.

For Further Reflection

- Why does suffering tend to isolate us?
- If God treated us fairly, what negative consequences would you have experienced recently?
- In your view, does freedom require consequences? Why or why not? How does freedom relate to the problem of evil and suffering?
- Is the promise of a future reward relevant to your present suffering? Why or why not?
- This chapter claims that God redeems all that he allows. Does this assertion help you with problems you're facing today? Does it bring up more questions?

CHAPTER 8

Did God Cause My Father's Death?

My father did nothing to cause his heart disease—he didn't smoke, wasn't overweight, and lived a moral life. I want very much to know whether God initiated my father's death or chose not to prevent its natural occurrence. The same question comes to mind whenever hurricanes and tornadoes leave a wake of destruction after a storm. Most likely you have experienced enough undeserved suffering to want an answer as well. But in order to find the answer, we need to examine some more big questions—about God's sovereignty and humans' free will.

Let me begin by typing some gibberish: a;sldkfjghfjfkdlsla;sldkfjfhgjfjdksla. I'm pretty certain no one knew I was going to type those letters until I did, and that in actuality, I could have typed something else instead, for instance: qpwoeirutyrueiwoqp. Some people say that

God chooses all that happens, and our apparent freedom as humans is only apparent. If God is truly the sovereign Lord of the universe, nothing can happen outside his perfect will, or so we're told. If he knows all that is about to happen, it must all be determined before it occurs. Just because we think we're free doesn't prove that we are.

How could that be true? Perhaps you saw the movie *The Matrix*. The premise is frightening: You and I actually exist in a colossal computer that uses our physical energy to power itself. It has created in our minds the illusion that we are living in our world and making free choices along the way. If the movie were right, how would we ever know it? If I'm dreaming as I type these words but think I'm awake, how would I know I'm not? If you're hallucinating at this moment, imagining that you're reading this book when it doesn't really exist, how would you know? It's at least possible that apparent freedom isn't real, that our imagined choices are all part of God's perfect and predetermined plan.

Other theologians say that God gave us freedom to choose, that our wills and decisions are real. But what does that assertion say about God's sovereignty? Perhaps he doesn't really see the future—but then how could he be the omniscient (all-knowing) God of the universe? Perhaps he allows us to make decisions that violate his will—but if that were true, how could he be the omnipotent (all-powerful), holy Lord of all that is?

It's all just an abstract theological argument until I ask this question: Did God cause my father to die? Did he cause my mother to have cancer? Did he cause 9/11, COVID, or the

October 7 attacks? If he did, what kind of loving Father is he? If he did not, what kind of sovereign Lord is he?

In the last chapter I concluded that God's holiness requires him to permit nothing that he cannot use to fulfill his perfect will. *Permit* is the operative word here. I am much more comfortable with a God who permits bad things he can use than with a God who *causes* bad things he can use. If he caused 9/11 or my father's death or Hitler's Holocaust, I want to know it. Until I do, it's hard for me to love him more intimately and trust him more unconditionally. I want to know who I'm dealing with here.

Don't you?

Everything Is Determined by God

When we start asking these types of questions, we enter a centuries-old wrestling match. Sovereignty (determinism) stands on one side, free will (choice) on the other, both engaged in a combat that has been waged theologically for centuries.

John Calvin (1509–1564) was a lawyer before he became a Christian (not to say that lawyers can't be Christians—that's just the order in which it happened for him). So when he embraced his new faith, he brought along an insistence on logic and consistency. His *Institutes of the Christian Religion* is still fundamental to Reformed theology, the doctrines that Presbyterian churches in the United States follow.

Calvinist theology is succinctly summarized in the five points adopted by the Synod of Dort in the early seventeenth century:

- **T**otal depravity: The fall of Adam and Eve affected every part of us, our minds and our wills.
- **U**nconditional divine election: We can do nothing to earn our salvation.
- **L**imited atonement: Christ died only for those *elected*, or chosen, by God for salvation.
- **I**rresistible grace: The *elect* will always accept the grace of God.
- **P**erseverance of the saints: Those who receive salvation can never lose it.

As you can see, the five points begin with letters that form the acronym TULIP. *Five-point* or *tulip* Calvinists accept each of these assertions, maintaining that God's will cannot be defeated if he is God. If he wants one of us to be in heaven, we will be there. In addition, they add, if God is sovereign over the future, he must know what choice we are going to make regarding salvation in Christ.

Most people hear this theological position and immediately respond that it's not fair for God to choose some people to go to heaven and the rest to go to hell. Calvinists reply that if God were fair, no one could be in heaven since "all have sinned and fall short of the glory of God" (Romans 3:23) and "the wages of sin is death" (Romans 6:23). In other words, none of us deserve to go to heaven; all salvation is by God's grace.

The critic replies, "None of us deserve heaven, but it is unfair for any to be chosen unless all are chosen."

This argument leads us to the other opponent in the ring.

Our Choices Are Our Own

Joseph Arminius (1560–1609) believed that God made us to worship him, but also noted that worship requires a choice. If someone drags you to a church service against your will, it's unlikely that your worship will be joyous. God wants us to use this freedom to choose to love and worship him. But those who make that wise choice retain their freedom and can later choose to use it against him. They can be saved and later lose their salvation. You can choose to be married and later choose not to be, or choose to read this book but midway through change your mind.

This theological approach accepts *unconditional divine election*, the idea that we don't deserve for God to forgive our sins and give us salvation. But as you can see, it doesn't accept the other four points of Calvinism. John Wesley and his followers were greatly influenced by Arminius's position, popularizing it through the Methodist movement.

Getting to the Heart of the Problem

I have struggled with this issue for years, eventually adopting a middle ground that makes the most sense to me. I agree that sin affects every part of our lives so that we are incapable of meeting God's perfect standards or earning a place in his perfect heaven. The Bible clearly teaches that all of us have in fact sinned and battle sin on a continual basis. The apostle Paul spoke for all of us when he said:

> I find this law at work: Although I want
> to do good, evil is right there with me. For

> in my inner being I delight in God's law; but I see another law at work in me, waging war against the law of my mind and making me a prisoner of the law of sin at work within me. What a wretched man I am! Who will rescue me from this body that is subject to death? (Romans 7:21–24 NIV)

Every day, in some way, my life is touched by sin. As much as I don't like admitting it, my body is decaying, my mind runs in ungodly directions, and I can be as emotionally volatile as the next person.

I believe that salvation is God's gift of grace, not earned or deserved by sinful humans. I didn't do anything to earn my relationship with God except ask for it. When I became a Christian at fifteen, I had only been going to church for a few weeks, didn't own a Bible, and had not put a dime in the offering plate. I had made no changes in my life whatsoever.

In writing to the Ephesians, the apostle Paul seems to believe that all people are like I was, no matter how many church services we attended before trusting in Jesus: "For it is by grace you have been saved, through faith—and this not from yourselves, it is the gift of God—not by works, so that no one can boast" (Ephesians 2:8–9 NIV).

Calvinists and I part ways with the idea of limited atonement—that Jesus died only for people who would trust him as their Savior and Lord. I understand the logic: God knew who would trust in his Son, and he would not waste his death on anyone who would not accept his love. If I invite our entire church staff to our home for Sunday lunch but know only six will come, my wife will not prepare food for the rest.

However, Jesus suffered the same death, whether it was for twelve disciples or two billion Christians today. "For God so loved the world, that he gave his only Son" (John 3:16). I'm not sure limited atonement is wrong so much as I wonder if it's irrelevant.

Irresistible grace—the idea that people chosen by God for salvation will in fact accept his gift—is something we'll get back to in a moment.

I accept the idea of the *perseverance of the saints* without question. Once I was born again as a child of God, it was impossible for me to go back to my condition before that event. My relationship with my Father is like my sons' relationships to me. My sons will always be my sons, whether they like it or not, whether or not they feel like it or act like it. Once they were born as my sons, they became my sons forever.

Arminians believe that I still possess the freedom to choose to reject Jesus, but I disagree. I no longer possess the freedom to be unborn, or to choose different parents, or to be African American rather than Anglo-American. Some choices are simply not available to me. The choice to rewind the tape and return to my preconversion state is among them.

Let's go back to the idea of God's irresistible grace. I thought I made a free choice on September 9, 1973, when I asked Christ to be my Savior and Lord. But maybe I was wrong. Maybe I would have accepted his grace eventually, even if not on that day. I cannot know for certain in practical experience—I cannot reverse time and refuse salvation on that day in 1973 to see what happens next.

The issue is somewhat irrelevant regarding my salvation, since that is a settled matter. But it is much more relevant to the decisions I make in the next minute and hour. It is a crucial question when asked about other events, such as 9/11 and the Holocaust and my father's early death.

Do the events of our lives just happen, or are they caused by God? Did God cause my father's death, or was it simply the consequence of living in a fallen world? Are our choices free or not? The answers will say much about the God who wants us to trust him unconditionally.

What Does the Bible Say?

The debate has gone on for centuries because there are passages in God's Word that seem to support each side.

Almost immediately Calvinists turn to Romans 9:18: "Therefore God has mercy on whom he wants to have mercy, and he hardens whom he wants to harden" (NIV). Here the apostle Paul was referring to Pharaoh's hardened heart during the Jewish enslavement in Egypt. In Exodus 7:3–4, God says, "I will harden Pharaoh's heart, and though I multiply my signs and wonders in Egypt, he will not listen to you" (NIV). Then four chapters later it says: "Moses and Aaron performed all these wonders before Pharaoh, but the LORD hardened Pharaoh's heart, and he would not let the Israelites go out of his country" (Exodus 11:10 NIV).

These statements would seem to end the debate: God clearly hardens the hearts of people he does not want to accept his word and will—in this case, so he could use the Exodus to liberate his people and show them his power and glory. God chooses some people to accept his love and others to reject it. But is the issue that simple?

In between the passages mentioned above, Pharaoh's hardened heart is noted in two more instances. After the plague of frogs ended, Pharaoh refused to free the Israelites. "When Pharaoh saw that there was relief, he hardened his heart and would not listen to Moses and Aaron, just as the LORD had said" (Exodus 8:15 NIV). The same thing happened after the plague of flies. "Pharaoh hardened his heart and would not let the people go" (Exodus 8:32 NIV). So did God harden Pharaoh's heart, or was the Egyptian leader responsible for his own sin? Both positions seem to be supported by the text.

Again quoting Exodus, Paul reminds us that God said to Moses, "I will have mercy on whom I have mercy, and I will have compassion on whom I have compassion" (Romans 9:15). He asks, "Does not the potter have the right to make out of the same lump of clay some pottery for special purposes and some for common use?" (Romans 9:21 NIV).

He seemed even clearer when he told the Ephesians,

> He chose us in him before the creation of the world to be holy and blameless in his sight. In love he predestined us for adoption to sonship through Jesus Christ, in accordance with his pleasure and will—to the praise of his glorious grace, which he has freely given us in the One he loves. (Ephesians 1:4–6 NIV)

At the same time, Paul assured Timothy that God "wants all people to be saved and to come to a knowledge of the truth" (1 Timothy 2:4 NIV). Peter agreed: "The Lord is not slow in keeping his promise, as some understand slowness. Instead he is patient with you, not wanting anyone to perish, but everyone to come to repentance" (2 Peter 3:9 NIV).

So which is it? Does God choose only some to be saved, or does he want everyone to be in heaven with him? The biblical answer seems to be yes.

This apparent contradiction is what logicians call an *antinomy*. If two statements are both true, we must accept them both even if they appear to contradict each other. It's actually hard to find a fundamental biblical doctrine that doesn't qualify. Is God three or one? Was Jesus fully divine or fully human? Is the Bible divinely inspired or humanly written?

It's possible to ask a question for which there is no answer—what philosophers call a *category mistake*. How much does the color red weigh? What color is the number seven? Can God make a rock so big that he can't move it? Or two mountains without a valley in the middle? Or a square circle? When my brother and I were young children, we would ask our mother which of us she loved the most. She was wise enough to change the subject.

There is a way to resolve the dilemma somewhat. The passages that seem to support Calvinistic irresistible grace at least indicate that God knows what we are going to choose before we choose it. But knowing is not the same thing as determining. Janet knows that every time we go to an ice cream parlor I'll order strawberry. She thinks it's a boring way to live, while I see it as one less problem to solve. The fact that she knows my choice doesn't mean she makes it.

I know my analogy breaks down—the next time I might order cherry ice cream just to confuse Janet—but it doesn't break down with God. Remember, he created time and he transcends it. If time is a line on a page, God is the page. He's not *looking into* tomorrow so much as he's already there. You and I are caught in the space-time continuum, but he's not. He sees tomorrow better than I can see today.

But that doesn't mean that he's already chosen what I'll do when it arrives. I can watch you read these words, but that doesn't mean I made you read them. Seeing and choosing are not the same. God can see the sermon I'll preach next Easter, but I still have to write it.

But we still haven't solved the problem. If God's omniscience means that he saw 9/11 before it happened, that's one thing. If his sovereignty means that he caused it, since nothing can happen outside his will, that's something else entirely. I can accept that God knew my father would die of a heart attack. If he caused it, I want to know why.

God Is So Sovereign He Can Choose Not to Be

Here's how I understand the relationship of God's sovereignty to my freedom: The Lord has chosen to give me free will so that I can choose to worship him. But knowing that freedom isn't free if it's determined, God honors the free will he gave me by limiting himself by my freedom.

This decision doesn't depreciate God's sovereignty, since he made free will himself. My authority as the pastor of our church is not lessened by my decision not to exercise it over every decision we make. If our deacons told me I couldn't choose the hymns we will sing next Sunday, that would be one thing. If I decide voluntarily to allow our worship pastor to make that decision, that's something else.

God wants us all to come to repentance (2 Peter 3:9) and salvation (1 Timothy 2:4), but not every person chooses to accept his love. He chooses to honor the free will he has given us, so that we can make this decision in complete freedom. So far, so good.

But what about events that occur without human choice? Victims of hurricanes and earthquakes obviously didn't choose to be victims. We can say that natural disasters are the result of the first man's (Adam's) sin, and we'd be right (Romans 8:20–22). But natural disasters don't result from your sin and mine. It would seem that God has also limited himself regarding the consequences of Adam's free choice to sin by allowing the natural disasters and diseases that it still causes.

Why, then, does God sometimes intervene when these devastating events occur? He clearly manipulated nature when he parted the waters of the Red Sea, when the Israelites crossed the Jordan River into the promised land, and when he resurrected Jesus from the dead. Throughout Jesus's ministry, he healed the blind and made diseased bodies whole. According to James, Jesus still heals today (James 5:13–16).

I understand that God allows the evil and suffering that result from misused freedom. And I can accept the premise that he permits nothing he will not use for his glory and our good. But does he *cause* these bad things to happen?

He certainly caused the flood of Noah's day to devastate the human population, and the Red Sea to swallow up the Egyptian armies. He will cause the plagues and destruction recorded in the book of Revelation. Does he cause all that goes wrong in nature?

Does God Cause All Natural Suffering?

Let's examine the issue by looking at the pattern of Scripture. Whenever God causes natural calamity or personal disease in the Bible, he always explains why. He brought about the flood because of the rampant sinfulness of humanity, and he gave Noah a century to warn the people before the rains came. He initiated the plagues of the Exodus in response to Pharaoh's sin and to show his people their God's miraculous power over the mightiest nation on earth.

He sent Joshua to destroy the Canaanites not only to give his people a land of their own but also in response to the wicked sins of those who inhabited it (Genesis 15:16). He raised up oppressors to persecute his people when their sins demanded such justice (Judges 2:10–15). He brought about the demise of the houses of Eli and Saul because of their sins against him (1 Samuel 2:30–36; 13:13–14). Each time, they were warned before judgment fell.

God's people were captured by Assyria and Babylon, but not before his prophets had predicted such doom if they did not repent. Because King Herod "did not give praise to God . . . he was eaten by worms and died. But the word of God continued to spread and flourish" (Acts 12:23–24 NIV).

A good father does not punish his children without explaining why. When my boys were teenagers, I would not have taken their car keys, simply expecting them to figure out what they had done wrong. Jesus taught us, "If you, then, though you are evil, know how to give good gifts to your children, how much more will your Father in heaven give good gifts to those who ask him!" (Matthew 7:11 NIV). So I can assume that my Father would not initiate physical death or pain to punish his children without telling us why.

God did not cause my father's death as punishment for his sins or mine. Over the nearly five decades since my father has been gone, God has never given me any indication that sin led to my father's passing. If my family is being judged for something we've done wrong, we certainly haven't been told what it is. God can indeed initiate natural disaster and suffering, but he always does it for a reason. Throughout the Bible, he told people what it was. Since his nature doesn't change (Hebrews 13:8), it seems reasonable to assume that he still tells people the reasons for their suffering.

Suffering for Good?

But what about suffering caused by God for the sake of spiritual growth? God required Abraham to offer his son Isaac as a sacrifice not because he wanted the boy to die but because he wanted Abraham to trust him unconditionally. God required his priests to step into the flooded Jordan River so he could show them what happens when God's followers trust him completely.

I think of that possibility with my father's death and all the innocent deaths I have witnessed in my pastoral ministry. In each case, did the loss occur in order to produce spiritual maturity in the survivors? Again, it seems in Scripture that God does not initiate such tests without making clear his intention. He can use anything that happens for our spiritual good (Romans 8:28). But when he intentionally causes suffering for such a purpose, it seems that he notifies those who are to grow as a result.

It seems to me that suffering is initiated by God as punishment for sin or motivation for spiritual growth only when he says so. He will not allow us to plead ignorance before him on judgment day. If we are intended to repent or grow as a result of something he has caused in our lives, we'll know it.

I can attest that every time I've experienced conviction or punishment for sin, the reasons for my suffering were very clear to me. When it seemed obvious that God led me into difficult circumstances for the sake of spiritual growth, I knew what was happening.

The summer I spent as a college student serving as a missionary in East Malaysia, I experienced the loneliest days of my entire life. But I knew going in what to expect, and that my Father wanted to teach me through that loneliness to depend more fully on him.

Our family has definitely grown spiritually as a result of my father's death. Because he had been the financial and emotional anchor of our lives, we had to trust our heavenly Father on a whole new level. In the weeks following my father's death, God showed me that he loved me even when

I was angry beyond words at him. God has given my brother and me a much greater sensitivity to those who lose someone they love, and my father's death has given me credibility in trying to help them. But our Father has never told us that he initiated this tragedy to produce such growth.

I believe God permits natural suffering and death, but only causes it when he tells us so. God did not initiate the innocent deaths I have witnessed, though he permitted them as a consequence of misused freedom in this fallen world. While the cause doesn't matter to the deceased, it matters to those who are left. I'm grateful that God my Father doesn't act capriciously and that he doesn't initiate innocent pain or death without a redemptive reason.

We Live in a Fallen World

God created our planet and allows it to function according to the laws of nature. In the Garden of Eden, Adam was told to work and take care of God's creation (Genesis 2:15). He and Eve needed food for sustenance, so God provided the trees of the garden. If Adam had fallen out of one of them and hit a rock, I assume that he would have cut himself. Since the fall of creation, natural disasters and diseases have been part of life. But they're not God's fault or choice.

In the same way, my father's heart disease was not caused by God but by our fallen world. A baby's death is not the newborn's fault, but the result of living in a world of disease and death. God permitted what he could have prevented for reasons we'll not understand fully on this side of eternity. But we do know that God did not initiate them.

I'm aware that critics may question the difference between *permission* and *initiation*. If God permits what he could prevent, isn't he as liable as if he caused the suffering in question? If I allowed a child to fall from a crib when I could have stopped him, I would be as guilty as if I had pushed him. If God permitted my father's heart disease when he could have prevented or healed it, isn't he as culpable for it as if he caused it?

Perhaps he's culpable, but he's not capricious. God does not cause pain without a perfect reason. And he does not initiate suffering unless he's given us the chance to know at least some of the reasons why. The rest of the time he permits the natural order to continue and redeems the suffering it causes.

God permits all that happens; otherwise he is not all-powerful. He initiates only that pain that he explains to those who suffer; otherwise he is not all-loving. And he redeems all that occurs in his creation; otherwise he is neither powerful nor loving. How could he do anything else and be our perfect Father?

Who's in Charge?

In summary, here's how I view the question of sovereignty and freedom. First, God permits or causes all that happens outside of human decision, either as the result of the natural processes he has created or his own intervention in his creation. The trees and squirrels I can see outside my window right now are the direct expression of his sovereign will.

Second, God has chosen to honor the free will he has given each one of us. He wants us all to be in heaven but knows that some people will refuse his love. His grace is unconditional but not irresistible.

Third, God permits or causes innocent suffering such as natural diseases and disasters. Unless he permitted or caused my father's early death, he has no power to permit or cause anything else in the natural order.

Fourth, he permits rather than causes that suffering that is not the result of sin or intended directly for spiritual growth. There are times when he does bring suffering as judgment on sin or to mature our faith. But God will tell us when our pain is intended for such purposes. So he permitted rather than caused my father's death.

Last, he redeems all he permits or causes. Because he is holy, he can allow or create only that which is for his highest glory and our best good. Even when I cannot see evidence of that good, I must trust that it exists now and in eternity. I don't have to understand every aspect of an airplane to get on one. I don't have to understand all the ways God is redeeming my father's death to believe that he is. Now I see God through a smudged, dirty window, but one day I will see him face-to-face (1 Corinthians 13:12). And be able to ask him some very hard questions.

Using What We Have Learned

When the tsunami strikes or the hurricane destroys everything we have and we are questioning God, how can this discussion help us in practical ways? Consider the following steps you can take in the storms of life.

First, utilize the *free-will* approach to examine the origin of suffering. Is there a personal sin to admit? Is this pain in some way the result of your own misused freedom?

If you are not sure, ask your Father. Take some time and invite the Spirit to show you anything wrong between you and God. Write down whatever comes to mind. This type of spiritual inventory should be a regular practice. Confess specifically and genuinely whatever the Spirit reveals to you. Claim God's forgiving grace (1 John 1:9). Make restitution to others when doing so benefits them (Luke 19:8). But do not assume that suffering is always your fault. The experiences of Joseph, Job, and Jesus are clear evidence to the contrary.

Second, consider the *soul-building* model: What can I learn from this situation? How can I grow closer to God through this pain? Try to be open to every source from which such spiritual growth can come—ask friends for counsel, seek the Spirit in prayer and Scripture, and worship God even (and especially) when it's hard. Stay close enough to Jesus to hear his voice and feel his transforming touch.

Third, think about the *future-hope* concept: How can God redeem this present suffering for future good? How can he use your witness to touch the lives of people you may not even know? How will he reward your present faithfulness in the future and in eternity?

You may not be able to see the future, but you can believe that it is real. One of my seminary professors explained the value of future hope this way: "Imagine that you are struggling financially (an easy thing for most seminary students to identify with). You're sitting down to a dinner of beans and hot dogs when a knock comes at the door. A messenger is there with a letter notifying you that a very wealthy uncle whom you had never met is expected to die in the next few days and you will inherit a million dollars. You return to your beans and hot dogs, but don't they taste better?"

Last, lay claim to the *present-help* model: Trust God's presence and strength in the midst of your pain. Know that he loves you, no matter how the world judges or treats you. He will always be your Father if you have asked Jesus Christ to be your Lord. Nothing can take you from his hand (John 10:28). He will enable you to withstand this trial until the day he takes you home to glory.

I cannot imagine how God could have arranged things better than he has. Given that we must be free if we are to worship God and love each other (Matthew 22:34–40), he had to give us freedom and then choose to honor it. The result is a fallen world filled with fallen people. He must permit these consequences and the natural suffering they produce, or we're not truly free. But since he wants to redeem his fallen creation, he must be free to act within it both to judge sin and to encourage faith. Since he is love, he must redeem all he permits or causes.

Now, how has God disappointed you? What undeserved suffering have you experienced? You can believe that our Father permits or causes nothing he will not use for his glory and our good, or you can believe that he is capricious, unloving, powerless, or nonexistent. You have no other options.

We can decide not to trust God because he has disappointed us. When a doctor's advice doesn't relieve my migraines, I could choose never to trust physicians again. But then I'll never know that I can.

It's a step of faith, to be sure. But my decision not to trust doctors doesn't hurt the medical community so much as it hurts me. Refusing to trust God with my unexplained pain doesn't hurt heaven so much as it hurts me. Choosing to trust God means that we might be disappointed by him. Choosing not to trust guarantees it.

I ended the last chapter with the story of a courageous young couple in my church who chose to turn their dying little girl over to her Father. The doctors told them that her disease may have been genetic in nature, but they couldn't be sure. The decision to have another child was agonizing beyond words. But they chose to trust God for his perfect will once again. If their next child died, they would believe that their Father had permitted only what was best. If their next child lived, they would praise him for such grace.

Trey is now over twenty years old and a daily gift of joy to this family. Their faith makes them heroes and models of courage to all of us who are privileged to know them. It was hard to trust God for their child's life, but they're glad every day that they did.

What step of faith is next for you?

For Further Reflection

- Some people believe that God determines everything that happens. Others say that our freedom is the final determining factor in our life experiences. What do you think?
- This chapter says that God has chosen to limit himself to the freedom he has given us. Do you agree or disagree? How is this argument relevant to the problem of evil and suffering?
- Do you believe that God causes all natural suffering? Why or why not?
- Do you agree that God warns his children when suffering is specifically the result of divine judgment? Why or why not? Can you think of any modern-day examples of this?
- Who in your experience has modeled faith in the face of personal tragedy? What have you learned from them about God's justice and love?

CHAPTER 9

What Happens to Those Who Never Hear?

I still remember reading a statistic on the unreached that staggered me: The number of people who have never heard the name of Jesus Christ has grown by one billion in the last century.[74] The majority of humanity has lived and died without ever hearing the gospel. That may be just a statistic to you, but I came face-to-face with some of those *statistics* when I went to East Malaysia as a young believer (see chapter 5).

We Westerners survived Malaysia Air Service to Borneo; the locals called it MAS for May Arrive Sometime. We spent much of the summer hiking through tropical rain forests, meeting people who had lived the same way for centuries. These delightful, gracious, loving people had never heard the name Jesus Christ, and most of them had never met a Christian before I crossed their paths. For every unevangelized

Malaysian I met, I knew there were thousands I would never meet. Many of them would probably die in a few years' time. What happens to them?

The *problem of the unevangelized* is really five separate but related problems:

- What happened to those who lived and died before Jesus died for their sins?
- What about people who have not heard that Jesus died for their sins?
- What about babies and children who die too young to know that Jesus died for their sins?
- What about people who are unable to comprehend Jesus's death for their sins?
- What happens to people who have heard that Jesus died for their sins, but live in a place where their accepting the gospel is unlikely? It's easy for me to follow Jesus in Texas, but it is much more difficult for people to serve him in Saudi Arabia.

This is a discussion for theology textbooks, you might say. Why is it an issue for someone struggling to be intimate with God? For this reason: If God sends billions of people to hell (or even allows them to go there) for rejecting a message they have never heard, what kind of God is he? Conversely, if people can go to heaven without hearing about Jesus, what kind of God would ask Christians to sacrifice and even die to tell them?

If either option turns out to be true, I still want to be a Christian. I'm not going to stop teaching or abandon the ministry. But it will be hard to be intimate with a God who seems to treat the world, or his own people, so unkindly. The great commission (Matthew 28:18–20) is supposed to be at the heart of Christian ministry and missions. If God is unfair in requiring it of us, what else don't we know about his character?

Being Ignorant About the Ignorant

At the end of the first century AD, 181 million people lived on our planet. Of that number, one million were Christians. The vast majority of the world was unevangelized when John finished writing the book of Revelation.

By the year 1000, there were 270 million people in the world, 50 million of whom were Christians, composing 19 percent of the world's population. By 1900, one third of the world was Christian, and one half was aware of the Christian faith.[75]

By 2020, 2.3 billion professed Christ, 28.8 percent of the world. Muslims have grown from 200 million in 1900 (12.3 percent of the world) to 2 billion in 2020 (25 percent of the world).[76] From the death of Christ to today, billions of people have lived and died without ever hearing the gospel.

How do Christians respond to this fact? As best I can tell, there are ten different ways that Christians answer the question of the unevangelized. Briefly, they are:

- *General universalism*: All people go to heaven, for God loves us all.
- *Christian universalism*: All people go to heaven, since Jesus died for their sins.
- *Natural revelation*: People are judged by the light they have.

- *Responsive evangelism*: God will get the gospel to those who respond to the light they have already received.
- *Divine foreknowledge*: God knows what people would have done if they had heard the gospel.
- *Supernatural evangelism*: God will use nonhuman means to get the gospel to those the church does not evangelize.
- *Eschatological evangelism*: God will give the unevangelized an opportunity to respond to the gospel after death.
- *Determinism*: People chosen by God for salvation will hear the gospel and be in heaven.
- *Soteriological agnosticism*: We cannot know what God will do with the unevangelized, so we must do our part to be obedient to the great commission.
- *Restrictivism*: Only people who trust in Christ can be in heaven.

The list can be viewed as something of a progression from people who believe everyone will be in heaven to those who think only the elect will be. We'll look briefly at each view, and then I'll build a case for the approach I think makes the most sense in resolving one of the most difficult problems Christianity faces.

General Universalism

The foundational tenet of *universalism* is that God's love requires him to bring all people to heaven, regardless of what they know about Jesus. If God is love (1 John 4:8), he must want us to be with him in heaven. He could not allow any of us to go to hell. Universalists say all Scripture must be interpreted in light of God's loving nature. I understand this sentiment and even wish it were true.

Universalists often cite Luke 3:6, quoting the promise from Isaiah 40:5 that when the Messiah comes, "all flesh shall see the salvation of God." In context, this statement occurs during John the Baptist's ministry. If *all flesh* means *all people* regardless of their response to God's revelation, why did John come "proclaiming a baptism of repentance for the forgiveness of sins" (Luke 3:3)?

It's true that Peter tells us that God "is patient with you, not wanting any to perish but all to come to repentance" (2 Peter 3:9 NRSVUE). However, he goes on: "But the day of the Lord will come like a thief, and then the heavens will pass away with a loud noise, and the elements will be destroyed with fire, and the earth and everything that is done on it will be disclosed" (v. 10).

A universalist must explain Revelation 20:15: "If anyone's name was not found written in the book of life, he was thrown into the lake of fire." And remember what Jesus taught during his ministry: "Whoever believes in him is not condemned, but whoever does not believe stands condemned already because they have not believed in the name of God's one and only Son" (John 3:18 NIV). Indeed, "no one can see the kingdom of God without being born from above" (John 3:3 NRSVUE).

Paul was passionately committed to the ministry of "speaking to the gentiles so that they may be saved" (1 Thessalonians 2:16 NRSVUE). He told the Athenian intellectuals gathered at Mars Hill, "In the past God overlooked such ignorance [idolatry], but now he commands all people everywhere to repent" (Acts 17:30 NIV).

I must conclude that it is impossible on the basis of Scripture to believe that everyone will be in heaven, or that anyone will be there apart from Jesus's atoning work.

Christian Universalism

Christian universalism says that everyone goes to heaven because Jesus died for their sins.

We're all familiar with Jesus's claim: "I am the way, and the truth, and the life. No one comes to the Father except through me" (John 14:6). This statement seems to rule out universalism of any kind. But Christian universalists put a slight twist on it: Jesus is the means by which all people go to heaven, *whether they have heard and responded to his gospel or not*. To a Christian universalist, "No one comes to the Father except through him" means that everyone comes to the Father through him. They seem to overlook John's later reference to the purpose of his gospel: "These are written so that you may believe that Jesus is the Christ, the Son of God, and that by believing you may have life in his name" (John 20:31). *Believing* is essential to having life in Christ.

The apostle John writes, "In him was life, and the life was the light of all people" (John 1:4 NRSVUE), for "the true light, which enlightens everyone, was coming into the world" (v. 9 NIV). That sounds like everyone has the light of Jesus, whether they know him or not. But John 3:18 is clear: "Those who believe in him are not condemned, but those who do not believe are condemned already because they have not believed in the name of the only Son of God" (NRSVUE).

The Bible seems clearly to rule out Christian universalism.

Natural Revelation

Proponents of *natural revelation* say that God has revealed himself through his creation and human history, so that we are saved or lost depending on our response to this revelation. Their proof is Romans 1:18–20:

> For the wrath of God is revealed from heaven against all ungodliness and injustice of those who by their injustice suppress the truth. For what can be known about God is plain to them, because God has made it plain to them. Ever since the creation of the world God's eternal power and divine nature, invisible though they are, have been seen and understood through the things God has made. So they are without excuse. (NRSVUE)

The Creator has revealed himself through his creation, so that all of us are without excuse if we do not trust in him. Thus our problem is solved—except that it's not.

If God judges us according to the light that we have, why did Jesus tell his disciples to go into all the world, preaching the gospel message? Why would Paul give his life to tell the gentiles about God's love if they already knew all they needed to know?

This approach does seem to answer the vexing question, How did people go to heaven before Jesus died on the cross? Melchizedek was "priest of God Most High" (Genesis 14:18) without any recorded interaction with biblical revelation. Moses and Elijah were in heaven before Jesus died for them (Matthew 17:3). How could his death be necessary for their salvation?

The simple answer is that God is not bound by time. His Son's death around AD 30 can be as effective for Abraham twenty centuries earlier as it is for us twenty centuries after. God could not expect Old Testament followers to know something that had not yet happened. So he judges them according to their response to his revelation so far as they knew it, saving them on the basis of Jesus's death centuries later.

What about people who lived after Jesus but knew nothing about him? Proponents of natural revelation say that they are no more to blame for their ignorance than Abraham was to blame for his. God could not expect them to know something they have not been told, so he judges them according to their response to his revelation as they have received it, as through nature (Romans 1). When people respond to the light they have, their faith makes them open to receive God's grace.

However, Paul made it clear that human wisdom cannot find God: "Since, in the wisdom of God, the world did not know God through wisdom, God decided, through the foolishness of our proclamation, to save those who believe" (1 Corinthians 1:21 NRSVUE). He also taught that the status of those who lived before Christ is not the same as those who live after his atoning work: "While God has overlooked the times of human ignorance, now he commands all people everywhere to repent, because he has fixed a day on which he will have the world judged in righteousness by a man whom he has appointed, and of this he has given assurance to all by raising him from the dead" (Acts 17:30–31 NRSVUE).

My conclusion? Today everyone is required to trust personally in Christ or be condemned (John 3:18). God judged those who lived before Christ according to their response to his revelation through his creation and messengers. But now, after Jesus's atoning work, no one can be in heaven apart from personal commitment to Christ. Nature and human wisdom can show us that God exists, but they cannot bring us to him.

Responsive Evangelism

Responsive evangelism claims that God will get the gospel to those he knows will accept it. I once heard a preacher promise that if a native in a jungle village responds to God as he is revealed in nature, "God will parachute a missionary into that village."

This approach vindicates God's fairness. He will not allow anyone who would be open to the gospel to be ignorant of it. If a man has not heard the gospel, that's because he will not respond to the gospel. The unevangelized do end up in hell, but God's character remains true.

Unfortunately, this approach does not solve all our problems. It can make missions less urgent—if God has guaranteed those responding to natural revelation a chance to hear the gospel, why do I need to tell them? If I don't go, the Lord is required to send someone else. My disobedience cannot harm the ignorant.

I'm even more troubled by the practical consequences of this idea. If we can measure the response of people to existing revelation by their resulting access to the gospel, we must conclude that more than a third of the world has not responded to the light they have. Remarkably, most of them live in the 10/40 Window, an area extending from 10 degrees to 40 degrees north of the equator and stretching from North Africa across China. As much as 97 percent of the people living in the least evangelized countries on earth reside in this geographical area.

And yet these are some of the most religious countries on the planet. A staggering population of 2.7 billion Muslims, Hindus, and Buddhists live in this window. Most who follow these religions do so with unwavering commitment: Muslims pray five times a day, Hindus live by their worldview in every dimension of their existence, and Buddhists follow the Four Noble Truths and the Noble Eightfold Path every day. It is hard to believe that virtually none of these people are responding to the light that they have. And yet the vast majority of these people have little or no access to the gospel.

A paltry 1.25 percent of gifts to Christian missions is focused on this region of the world. It would seem that these people are not being targeted for the gospel in the present or in the future. So is it a strange coincidence that the vast majority of those born into Muslim, Hindu, or Buddhist homes turn out to be the least responsive to the light that they have? At the same time, the vast majority of Americans are apparently responsive to that light, as virtually all of us have access to the gospel.

Of course, I would never claim that God would not or could not get the story of Christ to those who have responded to the revelation they have already received. But this possibility doesn't seem to be a compelling answer to our question. And if it makes us relax our evangelistic commitment, believing that God must send someone else if we don't go, it might actually do more harm than good to world missions.

Divine Foreknowledge

As the name suggests, *divine foreknowledge* embraces the idea that God knows what people would have done if given a chance to hear the gospel. Included in this group are infants, people unable to comprehend the gospel, those living in places where Christian converts are persecuted, and people who have never heard the gospel at all.

Several biblical passages seem to support this approach. Paul said, "Do not pronounce judgment before the time, before the Lord comes, who will bring to light the things now hidden in darkness and will disclose the purposes of the heart. Then each one will receive his commendation from God" (1 Corinthians 4:5). God knows the purposes of our hearts, and will judge each of us accordingly.

It is true that God knows us all intimately. For instance, the writer of Hebrews warned us, "Before him no creature is hidden, but all are naked and laid bare to the eyes of the one to whom we must render an account" (Hebrews 4:13

NRSVUE; see also 1 Samuel 16:7; 1 Chronicles 28:9; Psalm 139:2; Ezekiel 11:5; Matthew 12:25; Acts 1:24).

God knows the future before it happens: "See, the former things have come to pass, and new things I now declare; before they spring forth, I tell you of them" (Isaiah 42:9 NRSVUE). For example, Jesus died "according to the definite plan and foreknowledge of God" (Acts 2:23). God knew what Pharaoh would do even before Moses asked for the Israelites' freedom: "The LORD said to Moses, 'Pharaoh will not listen to you, that my wonders may be multiplied in the land of Egypt'" (Exodus 11:9). So it seems plausible that he knows what anyone on earth would do if they heard the gospel.

However, the Bible makes it clear that we must trust personally in Christ to go to heaven. Remember John 3:18: "Those who do not believe are condemned already because they have not believed in the name of the only Son of God" (NRSVUE). I also question the rational plausibility of this argument. Even God is not obligated to do that which is logically impossible, like specifying the color of seven or the weight of three. He is not required to make a square circle or a rock so big he cannot move it. Is it logically possible for even divine omniscience to know with absolute certainty what people would do with a choice they have not yet been given?

Assuming divine foreknowledge, it is a remarkable coincidence that people who would not have accepted the gospel happen to fall into the 10/40 Window, while people who would have accepted the gospel happen to fall into the Christian world. Virtually no one on Borneo would have accepted; virtually everyone in America would have.

And what about excessive evangelism? Almost everyone in Western Europe has access to the gospel, though less than 5 percent go to church and presumably only a small percentage of the population have trusted in Christ as their Savior. If God knows who would have responded and thus gets them the gospel, doesn't he also know who would not respond? Why does he "waste" the gospel on them?

The Bible clearly seems to warn us that not everyone will be in heaven. It also seems to state that we can go to heaven only by trusting personally in Jesus as our Lord and Savior. The options we've considered may be popular in a postmodern world that believes sincerity is the only test for truth we need. But don't try that with your medicine cabinet—prescriptions are not all the same. Don't try that with the keys in your pocket—locks are not all the same. And most of all, don't try that with your eternal soul.

Supernatural Evangelism

Proponents of *supernatural evangelism* say that the gospel will be given directly by the Holy Spirit to people unreached by humans. The Bible makes clear that God is quite willing to use supernatural means to reveal himself to us. Examples include:

- lots (1 Samuel 10; Acts 1:24–26)
- visions (1 Kings 22:17–23; Acts 16:9–10)
- an audible voice (Exodus 3:1; Samuel 3:1–14)
- dreams (Genesis 28:10–17; Luke 1; Matthew 1:18–25)
- angels (Judges 13:1–20; Luke 2:8–20)
- prophecy (Jeremiah 1; Hebrews 1:1)

- direct evangelism by the risen Christ (Saul of Tarsus, Acts 9:1–22).

In fact, we can argue that everything we know about God has come through supernatural revelation. His Spirit inspired the Scriptures (2 Peter 1:21) even as he created the ordered world that reveals his existence (Genesis 1:1–2). Jesus's birth was tied directly to supernatural revelation disclosed in Gabriel's visit to Mary. He would have been born to a morally suspect single mother except for the dreams given to Joseph. Jesus would probably have been killed by Herod except for another dream given to Joseph. If God would use supernatural means to reveal himself and his will to us, why would he not use similar means to reveal the gospel, the most important truth of all?

Thousands of Muslims around the world are apparently convinced that he does. In recent years, Christian mission organizations focused on Muslims have begun reporting a large number of supernatural encounters between Muslims and Jesus, usually coming in the form of dreams. One website devoted to Muslim evangelism tells story after story. For instance, one man dreamed the following: "Two angels dressed in white robes stood on top of the mountain. Jesus was standing between the angels. He left the angels and came to where I stood watching. As he approached me, I knelt down and he laid his hands on my head."

Another Muslim "dreamt he was sitting with his arms tied to a chair. Then he saw a man he recognized as Jesus coming. Jesus touched the ropes and they fell from his arms." Another reports, "In the dream, Jesus told me to come to Him and read the Bible and He would show me the way, truth, and the life."

> Still another says, "I went back to bed after a short prayer and saw a second dream. This time it was Jesus as I saw him in the *Jesus* film years ago and I had trashed his video. He was hanging on the cross, the nails were in his hands and feet, yet he was smiling at me and talking to me. Though he was dying he seemed so beautiful. The cross was huge and I seemed like a little boy. My neck was falling back trying to see the whole face of Jesus and suddenly a huge big circle of light came from above the cross and down upon me."[77]

Many such visions are reported after Ramadan, the Muslim holy month of fasting and prayer. Some lead to Christian conversion, while others encourage Christian converts in the face of persecution. If even one of these accounts is true, it would be enough to prove that Jesus is willing to use supernatural means to give his gospel to the unevangelized. If he would appear to some who have not heard the gospel, is it fair that he would not give all people the same opportunity to know about his love?

It is clear that God wants everyone to come to repentance (2 Peter 3:9) and salvation (1 Timothy 2:4). He must get the gospel to all people on earth before his Son returns: "This good news of the kingdom will be proclaimed throughout the world, as a testimony to all the nations, and then the end will come" (Matthew 24:14 NRSVUE). Our evangelistic failure cannot cause his program of global missions to be defeated. Surely he would use supernatural means where natural means have failed.

We can think of numerous examples of supernatural evangelism in the New Testament. The Pentecost evangelism of the first Christians was made possible by the miraculous work of the Holy Spirit in enabling believers to share Christ in languages they had not learned (Acts 2:6). Peter and John led a crippled man to Christ and witnessed to the city after healing the man's body (Acts 3:1–10). Healings by the apostles led to the conversion of many in Jerusalem (Acts 5:12–16). Simon the sorcerer came to Christ after witnessing the power of God through the ministry of Philip (Acts 8:12–13).

Philip's encounter with the Ethiopian eunuch occurred after "an angel of the Lord said to Philip, 'Get up and go toward the south to the road that goes down from Jerusalem to Gaza'" (Acts 8:26 NRSVUE). The conversion of Saul of Tarsus is an obvious example of supernatural evangelism accomplished by Jesus himself (Acts 9:1–9). "Many believed in the Lord" after Peter raised Dorcas from the dead (Acts 9:42). Cornelius heard the gospel as a result of Peter's miraculous vision (Acts 10:9–16, 28). The proconsul on Cyprus came to Christ after God blinded the magician Elymas (Acts 13:7–12). Crowds in Lystra listened to Paul's message after witnessing the healing of a man lame from birth (Acts 14:8–18).

Paul's evangelism in the West resulted from his Macedonian vision (Acts 16:6–10). The Philippian jailer came to Christ after the earthquake that freed Paul and Silas (Acts 16:25–

34). Multitudes in Ephesus came to faith after "God did extraordinary miracles through Paul" (Acts 19:11 NIV). In fact, it is hard to find an evangelistic event in the book of Acts that does not have a supernatural dimension.

At the same time, these events are descriptive, not prescriptive. No text promises such work by the Lord. We can find many examples of supernatural evangelism in the Bible, but no text requires us to expect God to do such work today.

Eschatological Evangelism

Eschatology is the doctrine of *last things* or *end times*. *Eschatological evangelism* (sometimes called *postmortem evangelism*) suggests that those who have not heard and/or responded to the gospel on earth will receive another opportunity after death. While this is probably a new and somewhat questionable idea to you, it's an approach that has been gaining popularity among theologians in recent years.

The logic is simple. As we've seen, God wants us all to be saved (2 Peter 3:9; 1 Timothy 2:4). His missionary purpose cannot be defeated: "The gates of Hades will not prevail" against the church and the gospel (Matthew 16:18 NRSVUE). He intends "all nations" to be his disciples (Matthew 28:19). So, if everyone does not hear the gospel in this life, they must hear it in the afterlife. There is no other way God can fulfill his purpose of giving every person a chance to know him personally.

God is the Lord of all time, and he can do whatever he wants with life on earth and afterward. If he cannot get the gospel to us while we're on earth, he will get it to us after we leave the earth. Once we step out of time, he has all the time in the world to show his love to us.

Those who advocate eschatological evangelism cite several passages in support of their thesis. Let's examine them briefly.

First, Paul told the philosophers on Mars Hill that God "will judge the world with justice by the man he has appointed." How could he be so sure? Because "he has given proof of this to everyone by raising him from the dead" (Acts 17:31 NIV). And yet *everyone* does not know about the resurrection. Even in their most optimistic expectations, Paul and the first Christians could not believe that every person would hear the gospel in the immediate future. What about people who would die before Paul or someone else reached them? How could God have given "proof of this to everyone" in this life? Doesn't this promise require an opportunity after death?

However, Paul said that God "has given proof of this," a completed action. It must be that the proof God promised is Jesus's resurrection: "by raising him from the dead." Paul did not guarantee that all people would know of this event, just that it would be proof to them if they did.

Second, Jesus claimed in John's Gospel:

> Very truly, I tell you, the hour is coming and is now here when the dead will hear the voice of the Son of God, and those who hear will live. For just as the Father has life in himself, so he has granted the Son also to have life in himself, and he has given him authority to execute judgment because he is the Son of Man. Do not be astonished at this, for the hour

> is coming when all who are in their graves will hear his voice and will come out: those who have done good to the resurrection of life, and those who have done evil to the resurrection of condemnation. (John 5:25–29 NRSVUE)

Jesus said that "all who are in their graves will hear his voice and will come out" (vv. 28–29). Does this promise mean that the dead will hear the gospel from Jesus? This statement is made in the context of Jesus's judgment (v. 27), so we can assume that hearing his voice relates to such judgment. However, the text does not seem to promise that they will hear the gospel, but only that they will hear his summons to judgment. Literally, "they will hear his voice and come out." The result of hearing is coming out, not coming to salvation.

Third, Peter tells us that Jesus preached to "the imprisoned spirits" (1 Peter 3:19 NIV). Does this mean that he shared the gospel with them after they died? Probably not. They "were disobedient long ago when God waited patiently in the days of Noah while the ark was being built" (v. 20 NIV), so this text relates only to a subset of humanity—those living in the time of Noah. While exploring this complex text in detail is outside the purpose of this chapter, the likeliest interpretation is that Jesus preached through the Spirit in the preaching of Noah, not that he gave this particular group of people an opportunity to hear the gospel after their deaths.

Arguing from Silence

A significant obstacle to eschatological evangelism may be the statement of Hebrews 9:27–28: "Just as it is appointed for mortals to die once and after that the judgment, so Christ, having been offered once to bear the sins of many, will appear a second time, not to deal with sin but to save those who are eagerly waiting for him" (NRSVUE). The passage indicates that death is followed by judgment, and it mentions no intervening opportunity to hear the gospel and be saved. However, it does not specifically deny such a possibility. The only thing it says for certain is that judgment follows death.

No passage in Scripture clearly states that Jesus is doing anything in the present except praying for us: "Because Jesus lives forever, he has a permanent priesthood. Therefore he is able to save completely those who come to God through him, because he always lives to intercede for them" (Hebrews 7:24–25 NIV). First John 2:1 also promises, "If anyone does sin, we have an advocate with the Father, Jesus Christ the righteous."

What does it mean for Jesus to be our advocate with the Father? At the very least we know that he is praying for us now. Is it plausible that he could also be our advocate when we stand before the Father after death? If so, could he be active in preparing us for that judgment by sharing the gospel with those who have not heard it? The text does not state that it is so, but neither does it deny this possibility.

As you can see, we're arguing from silence. Any theological principle whose best argument is that the Bible does not deny its possibility is not going to persuade many people. However, consider the possibility that we are asking a question that the early Christians did not try to address. Their Hebrew culture thought in practical ways. If we asked Paul what happens to those who haven't heard the gospel, he'd probably answer, "Go tell them. Don't sit there reading that book filled with speculation—answer the question by doing missions and evangelism until it doesn't need to be asked."

Our problem is that you and I live in a world dominated by Greek rationalism and speculative thought. We like our truth to be logical and noncontradictory. Doesn't it bother you that we don't have a complete answer to this issue?

We can follow this train of thought: God wants everyone to be saved, but not everyone will have a chance to hear the gospel in this lifetime, so he must give each person a chance after death. Eschatological evangelism is a rational proposition more than a clear biblical claim. But that fact does not make it either impossible or heretical.

Determinism

Calvinistic theologians believe in *determinism*—God intends only the elect to be saved. The unevangelized were not chosen for salvation and thus would not respond to it. We may consider it unfair that God chooses only some people for heaven. But at least we do not have the problem of God's fairness with regard to the uninformed, since none of them would have become Christians even if they heard the gospel.

Second Peter 3:9 says God doesn't want any to perish—a difficult text for people who believe that salvation is limited to those elected by God for heaven. First Timothy 2:4 also seems to contradict this doctrine, as it states that God "desires everyone to be saved and to come to the knowledge of the truth" (NRSVUE).

Calvinistic theologians argue that 2 Peter 3:9 is intended only for those chosen for salvation. When Peter says that God is "not wanting any to perish," he means only that God is not willing that any of his elect should perish. Peter's letters were written to those "who have been chosen and destined by God the Father and sanctified by the Spirit to be obedient to Jesus Christ and to be sprinkled with his blood" (1 Peter 1:2 NRSVUE). Second Peter was likewise addressed to "those who have received a faith as equally honorable as ours through the righteousness of our God and Savior Jesus Christ" (2 Peter 1:1 NRSVUE). The larger context of 2 Peter 3:9 indicates that Peter is still writing to believers:

> But do not ignore this one fact, beloved,
> that with the Lord one day is like a thousand
> years, and a thousand years are like one day.
> The Lord is not slow about his promise, as
> some think of slowness, but is patient with you,
> not wanting any to perish, but all to come to
> repentance. (2 Peter 3:8–9 NRSVUE)

Seen in this light, the text is a promise that the elect will never perish, not that the nonelect will hear and be saved. Here are my questions: If Peter was writing only to those who had already come to Christ, why would he state that God wants *them* "to come to repentance"? And why would he say that God is "not *wanting* any to perish," rather than promising that "none of you *will* perish"?

It seems to me that God is patient with his church, the beloved, to give everyone the opportunity to come to repentance lest they perish. His patience is tied to the church's unfinished work of global evangelism, as we reach those who have not yet responded with repentance.

The other text that seems to contradict determinism is 1 Timothy 2:4—God "desires everyone to be saved and to come to the knowledge of the truth" (NRSVUE). Calvinistic theologians will counter that *everyone* refers to *all without distinction*, not *all without exception*. In other words, God wants all kinds of people to be saved, without distinguishing between Jew and Greek, slave and free, or male and female (Galatians 3:28). If that is true, the text does not promise that God intends the gospel to get to every person, only every *kind* of person.

But Paul continues: "There is one God; there is also one mediator between God and humankind, Christ Jesus, himself human, who gave himself a ransom for all—this was attested at the right time. For this I was appointed a herald and an apostle (I am telling the truth; I am not lying), a teacher of the gentiles in faith and truth" (1 Timothy 2:5–7 NRSVUE). Once again, *ransom for all* must mean *ransom for all kinds of people* if the determinist is right.

This seems to be a forced interpretation to me. Paul could have said, "all kinds of people," if that was what he meant. He was not shy about speaking against class distinctions (Galatians 3:28) or on the subject of the elect (Romans 9–11). The natural reading of the text is clearly that God wants all to be saved. I don't think many people would read the text in the way the determinist does unless they first adopted the determinist's presuppositions.

If I thought the Bible teaches that God has restricted salvation only to the elect, I could then agree that the unevangelized are not a problem for God's fairness—if they would never have accepted the gospel, it's not necessary that they hear it. Of course, I would have a larger problem with God's fairness in choosing to limit salvation only to a subset of humanity.

Soteriological Agnosticism

The foundational tenet of *soteriological agnosticism* is that we cannot know what God will do with the unevangelized. (*Soteriology* is a theological word relating to salvation. *Agnosticism* literally means *no knowledge*, referring to a question for which it is impossible to have a complete, rational answer. Taken together, the terms describe a person who believes that we cannot know the ultimate status of the unevangelized.) In essence, let's just obey the great commission and leave the issue of the unevangelized to God. We'll do missions while believing everyone without Christ is lost, whether they are or not. If we did our work, the problem would be solved anyway.

And it would. For many, this approach is the solution. But some of us wrestle with sending our children into harm's way to evangelize an unreached people group. I know that we should be willing to obey the great commission, whatever the cost to ourselves or those we love. But if the unevangelized don't need to hear about Jesus in order to go to heaven, it's harder for me to imagine sending my son to risk his life in order to give them a message these people don't need to hear.

I admit that it's better to be agnostic about a theological question than to resolve the issue at the cost of heresy. I don't have to know how long ago God made the world to know that he did. I don't have to know when Jesus is returning to know that he is and that I'd best be ready. But I do need to know if God condemns the unevangelized for rejecting a message they've never received, or if he sends his children to give their lives in sharing a gospel the world doesn't need to hear. Either of these conclusions tells me something about the God who desires an intimate relationship with me. And maybe it reveals where my heart is too.

You may decide that soteriological agnosticism is the best of all the options: Leave the unevangelized with God and trust him to do the right thing. But before you do, consider one last approach and then an option that I think makes sense of this confusing debate.

Restrictivism

We have come to the position that most evangelicals would choose and many would insist upon: *restrictivism*. If we do not get the gospel to the unevangelized, they go to hell. But I still ask, How is that fair?

Don't get me wrong. There is no doubt in my mind that the Bible requires a personal commitment to Christ as the means of our entrance into heaven. Consider Paul's treatise on the spiritual condition of those who have not trusted in Jesus:

> You were dead through the trespasses and sins in which you once walked, following the course of this world, following the ruler of the

> power of the air, the spirit that is now at work among those who are disobedient. All of us once lived among them in the passions of our flesh, doing the will of flesh and senses, and we were by nature children of wrath, like everyone else, but God, who is rich in mercy, out of the great love with which he loved us even when we were dead through our trespasses, made us alive together with Christ—by grace you have been saved—and raised us up with him and seated us with him in the heavenly places in Christ Jesus, so that in the ages to come he might show the immeasurable riches of his grace in kindness toward us in Christ Jesus. (Ephesians 2:1–7 NRSVUE)

The gentiles were spiritually lost without Jesus (Ephesians 4:17–19). Unbelievers are spiritually blind (2 Corinthians 4:3–4). The lost must be converted, as God made clear to Paul: "I will rescue you from your people and from the gentiles—to whom I am sending you to open their eyes so that they may turn from darkness to light and from the power of Satan to God, so that they may receive forgiveness of sins and a place among those who are sanctified by faith in me" (Acts 26:17–18 NRSVUE). It is a tragic fact that those who have not trusted in Christ will be in hell upon his return (2 Thessalonians 1:6–10).

When the Philippian jailer asked the now-famous question, "Sirs, what must I do to be saved?" (Acts 16:30 NRSVUE), Paul did not tell him to respond to the light he had. He did not wait for supernatural evangelism to occur or trust this man to an afterlife gospel encounter. He and Silas were clear and compelling: "Believe in the Lord Jesus, and you will be saved, you and your household" (v. 31). Then "they spoke the word of the Lord to him and to all who were in his house" (v. 32). As a result, "he and his entire household rejoiced that he had become a believer in God" (v. 34).

Christians Must Share the Gospel

The New Testament insists that we share the gospel. Paul asked, "How are they to call on one in whom they have not believed? And how are they to believe in one of whom they have never heard? And how are they to hear without someone to proclaim him? And how are they to proclaim him unless they are sent? As it is written, 'How beautiful are the feet of those who bring good news!'" (Romans 10:14–15 NRSVUE).

Jesus prayed "on behalf of those who believe in me *through their word*" (John 17:20 NRSVUE, emphasis mine). Paul was frustrated by the Judaizers who had been "hindering us from speaking to the gentiles so that they may be saved" (1 Thessalonians 2:16 NRSVUE). Clearly we are called to share the good news, with no expectation that humanity can be saved in any other way than by responding to our message. But I still have a problem with its seeming unfairness. Limiting heaven to those we have chosen to reach and were able to persuade to follow Christ will drop the number who are in paradise astronomically. But, you may point out, in other times and ways God has saved only a few.

For instance, God "did not spare the ancient world, even though he saved Noah, a herald of righteousness, with seven others, when he brought a flood on the world of the ungodly" (2 Peter 2:5 NRSVUE). Even though Noah preached for a hundred years, presumably not everyone heard and rejected his message. And yet everyone was destroyed except Noah's family.

We think of the multiplied thousands of Egyptians who were killed during the first Passover and the Exodus. They were not complicit in Pharaoh's rejection of Moses's message, but they died anyway. Everyone in Jericho perished except Rahab and her family (Joshua 6:24–25). God commanded his people to drive out all the inhabitants of Canaan, including their innocent children (Numbers 33:52). The entire Hebrew nation suffered from Assyrian and Babylonian devastation because of their leaders' sins.

We could say that God allows people to suffer unfairly every day when others who could help them opt not to be involved. Unsanitary water kills millions. Contaminated food jeopardizes life and health. Americans have the knowledge and means to improve the conditions of suffering people around the world, yet God allows them to suffer because of our lack of engagement. If he would let such physical suffering take place, why not allow spiritual and even eternal suffering?

It seems unfair that the unevangelized will be lost, but if God were fair, none of us could be saved. He indeed wants all people to come to repentance and salvation. But just as he has limited himself by allowing us freedom to accept or refuse his grace, so he has also limited himself by giving us the freedom to evangelize or not. In both cases, the results of our misused freedom are not his fault but ours.

But I cannot help believing that there must be more to the story. Surely the God who is love cannot sit idly by and allow billions of eternal souls to go to hell through no fault of their own. Yet I conclude that restrictivism is biblical in its insistence that everyone must trust Christ to go to heaven. But as I wrestle with the issue of fairness for the unevangelized, I've come to what I believe is the solution.

Redemptive Eschatology

I must warn you: What follows is my personal opinion. It won't be found in any of the theological volumes, but it makes the most sense to me. We begin with the concept (discussed in chapter 7) that the holiness of God requires him to redeem all that he permits or causes. When we choose obedience, we share in that greater good; when we choose disobedience, we forfeit that good personally. But either way, God brings a greater good from present circumstances. How could hell be redemptive, especially knowing what the Bible says about it?

The Bible clearly states that hell is a place of permanent separation from God (Revelation 20:10). Unlike other suffering, this is not a temporary circumstance that God will redeem for a future good. We can understand how God might use cancer to cause us to grow spiritually or redeem a tragic death by bringing the person to heavenly glory. Paul writes that present sufferings are not worth comparing to the glory to be revealed (Romans 8:18).

But hell offers no such future hope. Those who are there are there forever. They will confess that Jesus Christ is Lord along with the rest of humanity (Philippians 2:10–11), but their confession will be too late to bring them to salvation. They will know that Jesus is the way, the truth, and the life (John 14:6), but they will be barred eternally from making him their way, truth, and life. How is this redemptive?

And how is hell redemptive for unevangelized people who had no chance to escape it? Their first opportunity to hear of Jesus comes when they are judged and condemned to eternal punishment for not accepting him as their Lord. How can hell be redemptive for them? Not only is it too late for them to learn from their mistake in rejecting Christ—even worse, they never made that mistake in the first place.

A Hell of a Place to Be

Hell is a real place, mentioned twenty-three times in the New Testament, fifteen of those times by Jesus himself. Jesus calls it a place of torment (Luke 16:23). It is described in the Bible as flames, fire, a furnace of fire, eternal fire, and the lake of fire (Luke 16:24; Matthew 13:49–50; Jude 1:7; Revelation 20:15).

Hell is also called darkness: "Then the king told the attendants, 'Tie him hand and foot, and throw him outside, into the darkness, where there will be weeping and gnashing of teeth'" (Matthew 22:13 NIV). In another description, one taken from the literal trash heap called Gehenna, Jesus said, "Their worm does not die and the fire is not quenched" (Mark 9:48 ESV, quoting Isaiah 66:24).

Worst of all, hell is separation from God (Luke 16:26). Remember Jesus's warning? "I will tell them plainly, 'I never knew you. Away from me, you evildoers!'" (Matthew 7:23

NIV). This separation is permanent (Luke 16:26), for it is the "second death" (Revelation 20:14).

But are these descriptions intended to be understood literally?

Many theologians across Christian history have said no, that these descriptions are symbols of a literal reality. Hell is literally real but figuratively described in the Bible, something like Jesus's self-description as the "true vine" in John 15:1. For instance, physical fire only works on physical bodies, yet Matthew 25:41 teaches that the eternal fire was first created for spirit beings like the devil and his angels. John Calvin, Martin Luther, J. I. Packer, C. S. Lewis, and Billy Graham all considered biblical descriptions in this way.

But let's not miss the point—hell is terrible. You do not want to go there, nor let anyone you know go there. To be absent from God, and from all that is good, for all eternity—that is hell.

How Could Hell Be Redemptive?

It seems to me that hell could be redemptive only if it is the place chosen by those who go there. If people decide that they do not want to spend eternity worshipping and serving God, he is gracious and redemptive in allowing them to spend eternity separated from him. We might even argue that heaven would be a worse hell than hell for such people.

C. S. Lewis makes this very argument much better than I can:

> I willingly believe that the damned are, in one sense, successful, rebels to the end; that

> the doors of hell are locked on the *inside*. I do not mean that the ghosts [his word for those in hell] may not *wish* to come out of hell, in the vague fashion wherein an envious man "wishes" to be happy: but they certainly do not will even the first preliminary stages of that self-abandonment through which alone the soul can reach any good. They enjoy forever the horrible freedom they have demanded, and are therefore self-enslaved just as the blessed, forever submitting to obedience, become through all eternity more and more free.
>
> In the long run the answer to all those who object to the doctrine of hell is itself a question: "What are you asking God to do?" To wipe out their past sins and, at all costs, to give them a fresh start, smoothing every difficulty and offering every miraculous help? But He has done so, on Calvary. To forgive them? They will not be forgiven. To leave them alone? Alas, I am afraid that is what He does.[78]

Calvin Miller agrees: " 'God, can you be merciful and send me off to hell and lock me in forever?' 'No, Pilgrim, I will not send you there, but if you chose to go there, I could never lock you out.' "[79]

Why would anyone choose not to spend eternity in heaven? That's precisely what the devil and his angels did:

> War broke out in heaven; Michael and his angels fought against the dragon. The dragon and his angels fought back, but they were defeated, and there was no longer any place for them in heaven. The great dragon was thrown down, that ancient serpent, who is called the devil and Satan, the deceiver of the whole world—he was thrown down to the earth, and his angels were thrown down with him. (Revelation 12:7–9 NRSVUE)

Many facing the judgment of God in the book of Revelation still do not repent: "They were scorched by the fierce heat, but they cursed the name of God, who had authority over these plagues, and they did not repent and give him glory" (Revelation 16:9 NRSVUE). The authorities knew that Jesus had been raised from the dead, but they lied about the resurrection and refused to acknowledge him as their Lord (Matthew 28:11–15).

It's hard to imagine that anyone would refuse to be in heaven, but people who understand and reject the gospel make that very choice every day. Milton said that Satan would rather reign in hell than serve in heaven.[80] While the Bible nowhere says that the devil will actually rule hell, the poet may have described the motive of all who refuse to call Jesus their Lord.

I can understand how hell could be redemptive for those who choose it, but not for anyone else. To be both fair and redemptive, God must have given everyone in hell the chance to choose heaven. This seems a compelling conclusion to me regarding the destiny of the unevangelized: God must give them a fair opportunity to trust Christ at some point that has not been revealed to us.

What About Evangelism?

The greatest problem I have with this proposal is that it appears to lessen the urgency of personal evangelism. Sharing the gospel is a mandate, not merely an option. But if God will reach those we do not, why does it matter that we pay a price to share Christ with them?

As I struggled with this question, I thought about people who are doing evangelism in parts of the world I cannot or will not reach. Missionaries in Sudan or Afghanistan are sharing Christ with people who will probably never hear the gospel from me. I am grateful to partner with them in world missions. Their effectiveness in witnessing to people I cannot reach makes me no less responsible for the neighbor in Dallas whom I can.

Perhaps we should see God as one of our missionary partners. He will get the gospel to people we cannot or will not reach, perhaps using supernatural evangelism and possibly eschatological evangelism. I must share Christ with everyone I can for the sake of their souls and my obedience. And I can trust that the God who is both just and loving will reach those I cannot.

So I don't believe that our job of evangelizing is done. We must do all we can to see that every person hears the gospel, risking not one eternal soul because we've come up with logical answers to a speculative question. Reaching the lost rather than speculating about them would be best for everyone, don't you think?

If I won you to Christ today, and the two of us won two to Christ tomorrow, and those four people won four more the next day, and so on, how long would it take for the world's population to come to Christ? Less than two weeks. Winning people who will win people was Jesus's plan for reaching the world. It still is.

For Further Reflection

- How would you respond to the claims of a Christian universalist?
- Is natural revelation relevant to the problem of the unevangelized? Why or why not?
- Critique the suggestion that supernatural evangelism plays a significant role in answering the question of the unevangelized.
- Some theologians believe that God will share the gospel with the unevangelized after their death. What kind of impact would that kind of thinking have on the priority of missions and evangelism?
- This chapter suggests that God reaches those we cannot or will not. Would this approach affect your willingness to sacrifice for the cause of world missions? Why or why not?

CHAPTER 10

Does Prayer Really Work?

I have to be honest: I am "altitudinally challenged." I don't just mildly dislike flying—I hate it. As a child, I was coerced to fly with my family in a friend's private plane. I threw up during the flight, and from that moment on, a pattern was established. I would prefer being the John Madden of theology—if someone gave me a Greyhound bus to travel the country, I would never set foot in another plane. How I would get overseas is another matter altogether.

The reason I hate flying is simple: I want to know why something is true before I trust it with my life. I certainly believe Jesus's words, "Behold, I am with you always" (Matthew 28:20 ESV). But I have no idea how a multiton metal monstrosity can climb to thirty thousand feet and stay there. As a small boy, I wanted to fly more than anything else in the world. I used to lie down in the grass and stare into the blue sky, jealous of the birds and clouds and Superman. I once carved a set of wings out of cardboard, taped them on my arms, climbed to the roof of our house, and jumped. Fortunately, it was a one-story house. I still remember how that episode ended, and I fear the same result every time I step onto an airplane.

It would help me greatly if I understood the principles of flight. If I knew why and how an airplane lifts off the ground and stays in the air, I would probably be able to look out the window from my aisle seat and stop digging my fingernails into the armrest. The more vital the subject, the more important it is for me to know why—even before knowing how.

So the *whys* of prayer are enormously practical questions for my soul. I imagine that I pray about as much as most preachers do. I participate happily in the various prayer meetings at our church. I pray in our worship services. I pray my way through an intercessory list regularly. I pray for my family daily. I prayed before writing this chapter. But sometimes there seems to be a spark missing. I feel like I'm running the plays the coach sends in from the sideline, but I sometimes wonder if we're winning the game. I pray, but I'm not always sure why praying matters.

It's that nagging question: If God knows what I need before I ask him, why ask him? When I pray about my son's safety as he drives home from college or my brother-in-law's upcoming surgery, I don't think for a minute that I'm informing the omniscient Lord of the universe that those two things are happening.

If prayer isn't information, maybe it's motivation. Maybe my prayer convinces God to do something he would not otherwise have done. But if keeping my son safe on the highway is the right thing to do, wouldn't God do it whether I asked him to or not? If I have to talk God into doing the right thing, am I more righteous than he is? Surely the Lord of the ages doesn't need a regular pep talk from me.

So if God knows my needs and wants to do the right thing, why pray? And if prayer doesn't change anything, why bother in the first place?

Another question is even harder to ask: How can I be sure prayer really works? I can remember specific times when I prayed for God to do something and it seemed that he did. Remember my earlier story about the church member who was given up for dead but came back to life on the operating table while we were praying for his life? Or the friend diagnosed with pancreatic cancer who was given a clean bill of health by her doctors three weeks after we began praying for her? Did our prayers actually have anything to do with these apparent miracles?

Perhaps God was going to heal the two people anyway. Perhaps their recoveries were the result of natural occurrences we don't yet understand. And what about all the people I pray for who don't get well, the marriages I ask God to save that don't survive, the situations that get worse the more I pray?

So if I'm not sure why I need to pray or whether prayer makes a difference, it's hard to pray with intimacy or passion. Prayer falls into the *why not* category—it's recommended and must be good if everyone agrees—like taking vitamins every day and changing the oil in my car's engine every three thousand miles. I have no independent confirmation that I would get sick if I skipped my vitamins or that my car would die if it went another thousand miles on the last oil change. But isn't it better to be safe than sorry?

After all, there's no significant downside. Vitamins and oil changes and times in prayer don't really cost much. The possible return on the investment certainly outweighs the cost involved. But such a calculated, rationalistic approach to prayer is surely far from the communion Jesus experienced with his Father or wants for us.

I've heard and taught for years that prayer is the way God feeds our souls. So I must get some answers on this issue before my soul suffers from further spiritual malnutrition.

Why Pray to an All-Knowing, All-Loving God?

When Janet and I were first married, I took charge of the family finances. My first banking venture as a newlywed was calling my bank in Houston to verify my balance in order to open a new joint account with Janet. I thought they said I had $140.00 in my account, so I wrote a check for that amount to open the new account. Unfortunately, it turned out that I had $104.00. So the initial check bounced, along with every check we wrote during our first week of marriage. I then made the wisest business decision of my life. I delegated the family's finances to my very astute wife, and she's kept us out of jail and accurately balanced ever since.

In the last twenty-seven years, it has never occurred to me that I needed to inform Janet about our finances. In fact, she knows more about our money than I want to learn. I'm also not compelled to question her bookkeeping and tax-preparation activities. I know that she wants what is best for us and will always do the right thing. (Now if I could just remember to tell her when I use my ATM card, all would be well.)

If I don't need to inform or persuade my wife about our finances, how much less do I need to discuss our finances with my Father in heaven? Remarkably, he knows even more about our money than Janet does. He knows everything we have, and everything we'll ever have, and everything we'll ever need. And he loves us so much that he chose to watch his Son die so we might live forever with him. Surely I can trust him to help us with our sons' college tuition.

Why pray, then, about money? Why ask God to help us pay the bills, manage our retirement, and be good stewards of our resources? If he knows more about the subject than we do, clearly we're not informing him of our needs. Jesus actually said that "your Father knows what you need before you ask him" (Matthew 6:8). If he wants the best for us, why ask him to do what is best for us?

Does Prayer Change God?

When we pray, God does things he would not otherwise have done. In this sense, does prayer change God?

Such thinking makes no sense to me. Suppose that God was not going to help me complete this chapter before I prayed, but now he will answer my prayer by giving me the words he wants me to write. Which was the right thing for him to do? Perhaps he was right not to help me write the chapter because I needed the soul-building experience of sorting through my own thoughts and struggling with my own abilities. Or perhaps he wants you to read truths that could have only been written through his inspiration. If that's the case, was it right for him to withhold his wisdom before I prayed? If it was right for him to withhold it earlier, why is it right for him to give it now?

There are numerous biblical references that seem to indicate God changed his mind in response to prayer. Think of Abraham's intercession for Sodom and Gomorrah, negotiating with God about the number of righteous people who needed to be found before God changed his plan to destroy the city (Genesis 18:16–33).

Other examples are even clearer:

- When Moses prayed for the nation as they worshipped the golden calf, "the LORD changed his mind about the disaster that he planned to bring on his people" (Exodus 32:14 NRSVUE).
- God told the prophet Jeremiah, "At one moment I may declare concerning a nation or a kingdom that I will pluck up and break down and destroy it, but if that nation, concerning which I have spoken, turns from its evil, I will change my mind about the disaster that I intended to bring on it" (Jeremiah 18:7–8 NRSVUE).
- When God showed Amos the destruction he planned for the sinful nation, Amos prayed for his mercy. Then "the LORD relented concerning this; 'It shall not be,' said the LORD" (Amos 7:3 NRSVUE).
- After Jonah preached to Nineveh, "When God saw what they did, how they turned from their evil ways, God changed his mind about the calamity that he had said he would bring upon them, and he did not do it" (Jonah 3:10 NRSVUE).

And yet the Bible teaches that God is *immutable*—that he does not change. For instance:

- "Jesus Christ is the same yesterday and today and forever" (Hebrews 13:8).
- "Every generous act of giving, with every perfect gift, is from above, coming down from the Father of lights, with whom there is no variation or shadow due to change" (James 1:17 NRSVUE).
- "I the LORD do not change" (Malachi 3:6).

If God does not change, how can he change his mind? The fact is that he doesn't, at least not in the way we think. The Bible uses anthropomorphic language to describe God's nature and ways—the only way we can understand a perfect, supernatural being. For instance, Scripture speaks of the right hand of God (Psalm 48:10), even though "God is spirit" (John 4:24).

In reality, God does alter his plans when our actions warrant such a change. He would have destroyed Israel except that Moses and Amos prayed for the nation. He would have brought judgment against Nineveh except that the people repented of their sins. Seen in human terms, he changed his mind. But it happened without human persuasion: No one told God to do the right thing that he would not otherwise have done.

We all deserve to spend eternity in hell, for we have all sinned and come short of God's glory (Romans 3:23). But God alters his response to our sin when we repent and trust in Christ. He does not change his character, but his action. We need to be exceedingly grateful for such grace.

So prayer does not change God in the sense of persuading him to do what he did not want to do or to do the right thing he would not have done. But prayer does cause God to change his response to the person who prays. The question is why.

Does Prayer Change Me?

There's no doubt that prayer is the way God molds and shapes my soul. Like a carpenter who has to get his hands on the wood he wants to sand and paint, God's Spirit must get into contact with me if he is to mold me into the image of Christ (Romans 8:28–30). It makes sense that I would pray to an all-knowing, all-loving God—not for his sake but for mine.

However, the Bible is filled with many instances where prayer changed *circumstances* as the result of the person who prayed. Moses parting the Red Sea or seeking food for the Israelites in the wilderness; Joshua marching across the Jordan and around Jericho; the Israelites repenting and returning to God, gaining his protection and blessing; Peter freed from Herod's prison as the early church prayed for him; Paul and Silas liberated in Philippi as they prayed and sang to God—the list goes on and on. In fact, it's hard to think of a significant event in Scripture that did not result in some way from prayer.

So we're back to our problem. Taking Peter's example, for instance, why did the first believers need to pray for the apostle in jail (Acts 12:1–18)? God knew where Peter was and presumably wanted to free him before Peter's friends asked him to. So what was the point of their prayers?

Prayer Prepares Us to Receive God's Grace

Praying prepares us to receive what God's grace intends to give. Have you ever been in a situation where you found out a friend needed help after the fact? It's frustrating, isn't it? If he had only asked you, you would have been happy to do what you could. Such a request would have enabled your friend to receive what you already wanted to give him. The same applies to prayer.

It seems like only yesterday when our sons were crazy about Teenage Mutant Ninja Turtles. (How anyone thought ninja and turtle should be linked together is beyond me.) My boys would often duel with plastic swords (I think they were pretending to be the turtle Leonardo), inevitably breaking them. I was always there to duct-tape the weapons back together, but my boys would say, "Me do it!" Even though I wanted to help and possessed clear superiority in duct-tape engineering, I was forced to watch in frustration as they used an entire roll on each sword. God knew how I felt.

Praying is not a work of righteousness or a legalistic requirement; it doesn't earn God's favor in any way. And prayer doesn't inform an omniscient God about our problem. Praying opens our hands to his help. It allows our Father to guide and bless his child. If I will not receive his grace, he will honor my refusal, but not without his pain and my loss. Then I have not because I ask not (James 4:2). But if I will knock, the door will be opened (Matthew 7:7)—not because I deserved God's favor, but because I was willing to receive it.

How Can Your Prayer Help Me?

So we pray because praying changes us and because praying enables us to receive what God wants to give us. But how do these ideas explain the value of praying for someone else? How can my prayer change you? Assuming that there are blessings God wants to give us but cannot unless we ask, how does it help you if I do the asking? If the Lord is waiting for you to seek his help, it would not seem to do him or you any good if I ask on your behalf. Don't we need to do the asking ourselves?

A while back, I got a ticket for an illegal left turn. For the record, there was nothing illegal about it. I am convinced that the policeman misinterpreted the sign, and that giving me a ticket was the only illegal part of the whole event. But when I complained to a lawyer friend and described my strategy for mounting an overwhelming legal defense, he smiled and said, "Please don't do that." He explained the whole business about due process, evidence, and the unlikelihood that I could convince a judge that I was right and a police officer was wrong.

My friend arranged for me to receive deferred adjudication, a fancy name for driving parole. So long as I didn't commit another driving transgression for six months, all would be well. But we had to go to the courthouse, where I had to stand in front of the judge and receive my sentence to complete the process. My friend knew that I was still mad about the whole thing, and that I had a speech all worked out in my mind. (There's no pain like that of an undelivered defense.) So as we walked together up to the bench, he kept whispering, "Don't say a word. Don't say a word." Thankfully I listened, only saying

"Yes, sir" at the appropriate times, and all was done. I've since served my probation and am an upstanding citizen again.

Despite all the ways my friend helped me, he could not stand in my place. Only I could exercise my free will and receive my sentence from the judge. It would seem that we are in the same position before the Judge of the ages.

And yet the Bible consistently endorses intercession and calls us to pray for others:

- Jesus "made intercession for the transgressors" (Isaiah 53:12 NIV).
- He said to Simon Peter, "I have prayed for you that your own faith may not fail" (Luke 22:32 NRSVUE).
- Jesus prayed for those who crucified him. "Father, forgive them, for they do not know what they are doing" (Luke 23:34 NIV).
- The Holy Spirit "intercedes for the saints according to the will of God" (Romans 8:27).
- Jesus "intercedes for us" now (Romans 8:34 NSRVUE).
- He "is able for all time to save those who approach God through him, since he always lives to make intercession for them" (Hebrews 7:25 NSRVUE).
- Paul wrote to the Romans, "I appeal to you, brothers and sisters, by our Lord Jesus Christ and by the love of the Spirit, to join me in earnest prayer to God on my behalf" (Romans 15:30 NRSVUE).
- The apostle assured the Ephesians, "I do not cease to give thanks for you as I remember you in my prayers" (Ephesians 1:16 NRSVUE).

- We are told to pray for all: "I urge that supplications, prayers, intercessions, and thanksgivings be made for everyone, for kings and all who are in high positions, so that we may lead a quiet and peaceable life in all godliness and dignity. This is right and acceptable before God our Savior, who desires everyone to be saved and to come to the knowledge of the truth" (1 Timothy 2:1–4 NRSVUE).

Is there any question that God wants us to pray for others and promises results for such intercession? But why? If prayer helps us receive what God wants to give, how can we do that for another person?

I understand the logic of praying for those who request our intercession. Paul asked the Romans to pray to God on his behalf; James prayed on behalf of the sick who presumably acknowledged their condition and need for divine help. We can assume that when Peter was in jail, he was receptive to the miraculous aid for which the church prayed (Acts 12).

So we could certainly conclude that intercession makes sense so long as the people for whom we pray either request our prayer or are open to its results. But Paul instructed Timothy to pray "for kings and all who are in high positions" (1 Timothy 2:2). Is it likely that the emperors of the Roman Empire knew about these prayers or even welcomed them? The emperor for whom Paul sought intercession would one day behead him for his trouble.

And why should we pray for lost people who are not seeking the Lord? How can God bring them to faith without violating their freedom? On the other hand, if he cannot save their souls as a result of our prayers, why pray?

I could understand praying for others in a way that would benefit me. So long as I want the results of my prayers, God is not violating my freedom by granting them to me. But he is presumably violating the freedom of those for whom I pray, if they then act in unplanned ways that benefit me.

And yet I find myself praying like this all the time. For instance, how was God going to answer my prayers for my sons to excel at basketball? Was he going to block their opponents' shots from going in the basket? (It is likely that their parents were praying at the same time for their sons' success and my sons' consequent failures.) In order for the Lord to help improve my sons' academic class rankings, he would need to stop helping (and might even need to hinder) the students they displace, apparently violating their freedom.

For God to enable Ryan and Craig to receive college scholarships would require him to persuade the financial aid officer to favor them (perhaps despite that person's free will), with the possible result that another student did not receive that help. If God answered my prayers, how could he honor their freedom at the same time? How can God be fair in answering such prayers?

Here's the only answer that makes sense to me: When my prayer involves people who do not know me or do not welcome my intercession, God must answer my prayer without violating their freedom or treating them unfairly. So he will do everything he can do, short of that result.

In the case of people who are spiritually lost, God will answer my prayers by bringing willing Christians into their lives and inspiring their words and witness. His Spirit will convict the spiritually lost of their sins and need for salvation. And he will use and even engineer circumstances that may help them to be more open to his grace.

For instance, my wife's first introduction to the gospel came when she found a Bible tract on the ground and read it. We both believe that God arranged for a Christian to place it there. In this situation, God did not violate the freedom of the lost (Janet) or the freedom of the ones he used to help her come to faith.

As far as interceding for people who are either unaware of or unappreciative of my prayers, I can trust God to work in the same ways. He will use Christians who are open to his leading to take the next step; his Spirit will convict and work in the hearts of the strangers I am praying for. He will use circumstances to accomplish his perfect will.

When my prayers involve those who did not choose to participate in them, once again God will not violate their freedom or treat them unfairly. He might help my sons play their best game or write their best essay, but not at the expense of others. God has chosen to limit himself to the freedom he has given us. And his holiness requires him to do what is right—always.

So Why Pray?

In understanding the logic of praying to an all-knowing, all-loving God, I think we can say that (1) praying changes us, as the Holy Spirit uses our communion with God to mold us into the image of Christ; (2) praying positions us to receive what God's grace intends to give; and (3) praying for other people or in ways that involve others will bring results insofar as God does not violate their freedom or treat them unfairly.

These seem to be the rules of the game. Like all rules, knowing them doesn't keep me from playing—it helps me to play better. But I have more questions: Why doesn't God always give me what I pray for? Does God hear everyone's prayers, including those of Muslims and followers of other religions? What does God do when you and I are both praying for the same job? We'll ask him in the next chapter.

For Further Reflection

- Do you think that prayer changes God? Why or why not?
- How does praying prepare you to receive what God intends to give you?
- The chapter suggests that intercessory prayer cannot violate the freedom of the person for whom you're praying. Will that change the way you pray for people? How so?
- After reading this chapter, are you excited about praying more? Why or why not?

CHAPTER 11

Why Doesn't God Always Give Us What We Ask For?

I became a Christian at the age of fifteen. Within a few weeks, I began attending our church's Wednesday night prayer meeting. Our pastor would read over the hospital list each week, and then we would begin a season of prayer, as he called it. He would ask someone (usually an elderly deacon with a loud voice) to begin our prayers for the sick. Two or three others would rise to their feet to continue the prayer time. The pastor would finally kneel and conclude our intercession.

This was all very new and exciting for me. To think that God would heal people in hospitals just because we prayed for them was an amazing concept. I returned to prayer meeting the next week to see what had happened. Sadly and almost without fail, the news wasn't good. Despite our fervent prayers (many of them uttered in King James English), most of the patients did not get better, and some even died.

I assumed that this was just the way it was with prayer: You win some and you lose some. But then our youth group began to study the book of James. Reading ahead, I encountered this passage:

> Are any among you sick? They should call for the elders of the church and have them pray over them, anointing them with oil in the name of the Lord. The prayer of faith will save the sick, and the Lord will raise them up, and anyone who has committed sins will be forgiven. Therefore confess your sins to one another and pray for one another, so that you may be healed. The prayer of the righteous is powerful and effective.
>
> Elijah was a human like us, and he prayed fervently that it might not rain, and for three years and six months it did not rain on the earth. Then he prayed again, and the heaven gave rain, and the earth yielded its harvest. (James 5:14–18 NRSVUE)

"Anoint them with oil in the name of the Lord"? I had no idea what that meant, and to be honest, I kept thinking, *How are we going to smuggle a can of motor oil into the hospital room?* I also didn't understand the promise, "the prayer of faith will save the sick, and the Lord will raise them up." God hadn't done that for most of the people on our prayer list.

More than three decades later, I still face the same problem. Our congregation's hospital list is longer than the one in my small home church, but its members don't seem to benefit any more from our Wednesday prayer meetings than did those in the first prayer meetings I attended.

Since those early days of my faith, I have discovered more promises of answered prayer:

> Ask, and it will be given to you; search, and you will find; knock, and the door will be opened for you. For everyone who asks receives, and everyone who searches finds, and for everyone who knocks, the door will be opened. (Matthew 7:7–8 NRSVUE)

> If you have faith and do not doubt, not only will you do what has been done to the fig tree, but even if you say to this mountain, "Be lifted up and thrown into the sea," it will be done. Whatever you ask for in prayer with faith, you will receive. (Matthew 21:21–22 NRSVUE)

> I will do whatever you ask in my name, so that the Father may be glorified in the Son. (John 14:13 NRSVUE)

> If in my name you ask me for anything, I will do it. (John 14:14 NRSVUE)

> And this is the boldness we have in him,
> that if we ask anything according to his will,
> he hears us. And if we know that he hears us
> in whatever we ask, we know that we have
> obtained the requests made of him. (1 John
> 5:14–15 NRSVUE)

As I have studied these passages, I have decided that there are more principles to effective prayer than I actually thought I knew. As we discovered in the last chapter, biblical principles do not hinder our prayers. Like lanes on the freeway, they direct us where we want to go.

Keys to Answered Prayer

Think of the principles as keys to the throne room of God. When I turn a key in a lock, I do not earn the right to enter, but merely meet the conditions required. This is not legalism—I am still admitted to the presence of God by his grace. But there are some things I must do first.

Taking the promises listed above in order, first we must *pray continually*. In the original Greek, Jesus's statement can be translated, "Ask and keep on asking . . . search and keep on searching . . . knock and keep on knocking" (Matthew 7:7). It's not because continued prayer wears God down or earns his favor. Rather, it's because continued prayer keeps us in position to be molded by his Spirit, and it allows him time to engineer circumstances and motivate people to answer our requests.

I know a man who prayed for months that God would give him a new and better job. For a long time it seemed that his prayers fell on deaf ears, but he kept praying. Now that his new job is a reality, we know why the process took so long. A man in the home office needed to retire, so a man in the Dallas office could take his place, so that man's job could be available for my friend. Keep in mind that there may be more dominoes behind the only one you can see.

Second, we are to *pray in faith* (Matthew 21:21–22). Not because our faith earns God's answers, but because it is necessary for receiving them. Let's say that I wanted to give you the book you're reading. You'd need a certain amount of faith to accept it from me. I could have stolen it from someone who will now blame you. I could accuse you of stealing it from me. I could send you an exorbitant bill later. Your faith did not earn the book, but it was needed for you to receive what I wanted to give. In the same way, we must believe that God will answer us so that he can do so. He cannot give what we are unwilling to receive.

Third, we are to *pray for God's glory* (John 14:13). God will not share his glory, because it is impossible for him to do so. It would be idolatry for him to glorify anyone or anything above himself. This fact does not make him a cosmic egotist—he knows that seeking his glory is what's best for us. Philosopher Friedrich Nietzsche was right: The *will to power* is the basic drive of fallen human nature. The first temptation was to "be like God" (Genesis 3:5). It is still the basic strategy of Satan because it still works. Human nature doesn't change.

But when we seek God's glory before our own, we put ourselves in the proper relationship of creatures before our Creator. We enable our God to act as our Father with his children. We follow so he can lead, we receive so he can give, and we trust so he can bless.

Discovering this principle changed my prayer life radically. I used to pray for a hospitalized church member to get well. Now I pray for God to be glorified in this person's life. If he would be most glorified by healing her, I pray that he would. If he would be most glorified by helping her deal with her illness in victorious faith, I pray for that result.

Right now, I am praying that God would be glorified through the next words I write. If I am seeking my honor, I am not seeking his. And anyone who's ever tried to write or speak knows that if we're thinking about impressing people, we're not doing our job. The paradox is that they'll be far more impressed with us if we glorify God than if we glorify ourselves.

Fourth, we are told to *pray in Jesus's name* (John 14:14). When I first began attending my church's Wednesday prayer meeting as a new Christian, I was surprised to hear every prayer end "in Jesus's name." I had no idea what the phrase meant, but since everyone else obviously did, I kept my ignorance to myself. I soon began adding this phrase as a kind of magic incantation, figuring that it must work or people wouldn't use it.

Over time I learned why we are to pray in this way. Names are important in the Bible. God changed Abram's name to Abraham to tell the world that he would be a father of many nations. He changed Jacob (deceiver) to Israel (one who wrestles with God). Jesus changed Simon (sandy) to Peter (rocky). In the same way, "Jesus's name" is a biblical way of referring to his character, authority, and merit.

When we pray in his name, we are signing his name to our check, drawing on his bank account. If I wrote a million-dollar check to our church, they'd laugh and toss it in the trash. If Bill Gates signed a check with that many zeros, they'd race to the bank to deposit it.

When we pray in Jesus's name, we are asking God to answer our prayers on the basis of Jesus's atonement and love for us. We're not praying in our merit, as though we deserved to be heard and helped. Even though I'm a Baptist pastor, I have no more authority with God than anyone else. He knows every sin I've ever committed and every sin I don't know I'm going to commit. If I ask him to answer my prayers because I've earned the attention of the holy God of the universe, I'm wasting his time and mine. But when I pray for his help on the basis of Jesus's death and love for me, I'm speaking words that the Father loves to hear.

Finally, we are taught to *pray according to God's will* (1 John 5:14–15). This principle is too important to overstate. Asking my dad for a new car didn't obligate him to buy it for me. Even if I asked continually, believing that he would give it to me, promising to honor him for doing so, asking on the basis of his love and not my good deeds, he wouldn't buy me the car unless it was already his will to do so. (Sadly, it wasn't.) Such was his prerogative as a father.

With a human father, this principle may not be good news. Your dad could be stingy or overly demanding. Or he could be generous in a way that hurts more than it helps. My proclivity is to give our sons—and, even more so, our grandchildren—whatever they ask for, even if they would be better off earning the money to buy it themselves. Fortunately, my wise wife thinks otherwise.

The good news is that our heavenly Father always wants what is for our best. He loves us and likes us. He knows the past and the future better than we know the present. We can count on him to do the right thing every time.

How can we know what that is? One way is to search for a biblical principle that can guide our prayer. For instance, if I'm praying for a person to become a Christian, I know that I'm praying in God's will, since God "desires everyone to be saved and to come to the knowledge of the truth" (1 Timothy 2:4 NRSVUE). But if I'm praying for financial wealth, I cannot claim such a biblical guarantee.

At the same time, we should pray specifically rather than generally. Simply asking for God's will to be done is not sufficient. Jesus's prayer in the garden of Gethsemane is a great example to follow. First, we should tell the Lord what we want him to do. Then, we should submit our requests to his will, knowing that he will do what most glorifies him and is for our greatest good.

A Crucial Fact

This principle leads to one final key to answered prayer: *know that God will give you what you ask or whatever is best.* Why doesn't God always answer our prayers the way we want? Because he knows what is best for us. He never stops being a Father. Ask any parent about times when they decided not to give their children what they wanted because they loved them too much.

I can remember one day when my sons were young and I was outside scraping paint off a window with a single-edged razor blade. One son threw a tantrum when I wouldn't let him touch the shiny new toy I was "playing" with. Billy Graham was devastated that the girl he loved rejected his proposal of marriage, and he couldn't understand why God hadn't answered his prayers. Then he met Ruth Bell, and the rest is history.

We are seldom good judges of what is for our eternal best. I could not understand why God would call me from the faculty of Southwestern Seminary into the pastorate, but for four decades I've been glad that he did. Our family could not have been happier in Midland when he called us to Atlanta, or happier in Atlanta when he called us to Dallas. But looking back I can see that he knew better than we did each time.

I still struggle with God not answering my prayers for my father's health in the way I wanted. But as we have seen, God's holiness requires him to redeem all that he permits or causes. He must have permitted my father's death for a greater purpose that I cannot yet comprehend. Neither my father nor I misused our freedom to violate God's will for us. So I must conclude that it was best for my heavenly Father to allow my father to die. One day I'll understand why, and that fact sustains me right now.

So now I rest in the knowledge that God will always give me what I ask—or something better. As long as I keep praying with the faith to receive his answers, seeking his glory, according to Jesus's merit, in keeping with his will, I am in position to receive all that his grace intends to give. Whether I know it at the moment or not, he answers my prayers every time.

Does God Hear Everyone's Prayers?

One last question about prayer has troubled me over the years: Does God hear everyone's prayers? Can he? We've discovered that the principles for answered prayer clearly require that we follow Jesus. But how can we pray in faith unless we first have faith? How can we pray in Jesus's name unless we first trust in his name?

Does God hear the prayers of people who are not yet Christians? What about the prayers of children or of Jews, Muslims, Hindus, and Buddhists? What about the prayers of lost people? If he doesn't, how can they ever pray to become Christians?

And how does God answer conflicting prayers? The farmer prays for rain at the same time the golfer prays for sunshine. You're praying for your kids to win the soccer game against my kids' team, while I'm praying for my kids to outscore yours. Or both of us are asking God to give us the same job. Or maybe we're pastors of neighboring churches, each praying for the same family to join our congregation. (That happens more than we probably know in Texas, where churches are so numerous they sometimes share parking lots.) In short, does God answer everyone's prayers?

Praying to Become a Christian

Let's begin with the prayers of people seeking salvation in Christ. If Jesus heard and granted the request of the believing thief on the cross (Luke 23:42–43), I can be certain that he heard and answered my request for salvation when I first prayed it. But since I was spiritually dead through my trespasses and sins before I became a Christian (Ephesians 2:1), how could I have the faith to seek this salvation?

The answer is that God gives us that kind of faith when we respond to his Spirit's convicting work in our lives. Some theologians call this *prevenient grace*, the idea that God gives us the grace and faith to seek him. Others in the Calvinist tradition believe that God hears the saving prayers only of the elect, and that he enables them to pray those prayers. Either way, we can know that God enables us to pray when we seek salvation in Christ, and that he hears that prayer in grace.

Praying as a Non-Christian

What about the prayers of nonbelievers who are not choosing to follow Jesus? The question of children's prayers seems relatively easy. Jesus held up a child as an example of the kingdom of God, and he told us to become as children to enter that kingdom (Matthew 18:1–5). Until a child sins by consciously choosing to disobey God's Word and will, they are in unbroken fellowship with the Father. The prayers of children may therefore be the most powerful and effective petitions God hears.

What about Jews? They pray to the same God of Abraham as we do. But they do not pray to him through Jesus. Scripture is clear on the necessity of trusting the Son to know the Father:

> Whoever has the Son has life; whoever does not have the Son of God does not have life. (1 John 5:12)

> Every spirit that does not confess Jesus is not from God. (1 John 4:3)

> No one who denies the Son has the Father; everyone who confesses the Son has the Father also. (1 John 2:23 NRSVUE)

Jesus told us that no one could come to the Father except through him (John 14:6). If we do not trust Jesus as our Lord, we clearly cannot come to his Father in prayer. God loves the Jewish people so much that he sent his Son to die for their sins. But they must accept his grace before they can experience it.

What about Muslims? After 9/11 it quickly became conventional wisdom that Muslims, Jews, and Christians all worship the same God. Muslims in fact claim that Allah (the Arabic word for God) is the true God of Abraham and Jesus. For instance, the Qur'an teaches, "Say ye: 'We believe in God, and the revelation given to us, and to Abraham, Isma'il, Isaac, Jacob, and the Tribes, and that given to Moses and Jesus.'"[81] I have heard many Muslim clerics state that Muslims worship the same God as Jews and Christians do.

However, it is possible to use the same vocabulary but a different dictionary. The Muslim view of God explicitly repudiates the Trinity, and thus rejects the God of the Bible and the Christian faith. The Qur'an is clear on this question: "Christ Jesus the son of Mary was no more than an apostle of God. . . . Say not 'Trinity': desist: it will be better for you: for God is one God: glory be to Him."[82] Muslims absolutely deny the divinity of Christ and Christianity's central claim that Jesus is Lord.

So they do not worship our God. Since they do not pray to the Father through the Son, they do not approach God biblically. As a result, their prayers cannot be heard, even though God loves them and wants them to come to repentance and eternal life (John 3:16). The same holds true for followers of any religion that does not worship Christ as Lord.

Praying for Sunshine or Rain

How does God handle competing requests? My mother's family is related to Robert E. Lee, a fact that stood me in good stead when I was a pastor in Atlanta. Pastors on both sides of the Civil War were convinced that their cause was just. It is said that when a woman assured President Lincoln that God was on their side, he replied in great wisdom, "Better that we pray to be on his."

I'll bet that God deals with these kinds of prayers more often than we know. Not only when fans on both sides of the field are assaulting heaven with their impassioned pleas for victory, or when soldiers from both armies pray for victory in the same battle. Rarely does a prayer only affect the one who prays it. This is one of a thousand reasons why I'm glad God is God and I'm not.

Let's look at three facts that may be helpful in understanding how God can give every prayer his undivided attention. First, *God does not live in time as we do.* He created the space-time continuum and transcends what he created. So he literally has all of eternity to hear and answer your next prayer and mine as well.

Second, *the Lord can answer our prayers for events that occurred before we prayed.* Let's say you had some medical tests done this morning and are praying for good results this afternoon. In chronological time your prayer is illogical, since your test results are already determined. But God knew before time began that you would pray this afternoon, so he answered those prayers earlier, before you actually prayed them. It's never too late or too soon to pray to a Father like this.

Third, *God's character ensures that he will do the right thing every time.* If it is best for you to get the job I'm praying for, that's what God will do. He will always give us what we ask or something better. There are no losers when everyone prays. The team that loses is better off than if it had won the game. When a family moves from one church to another, both congregations profit more than they may know.

This is not fatalism or "the best of all possible worlds" naivete. As we have seen repeatedly, God's holiness requires him to redeem all that he permits or causes. He must always do what is best and right. When the farmer's prayers for rain are answered at the expense of the golfer's tee time, the golfer needed to be at home doing chores anyway.

Why Keep Praying?

I knew some of what I've discussed in this chapter before I began to write it. I had already come to the conclusion that God gives us what we pray for or whatever is best. Years ago I discovered the biblical keys to answered prayer, and I have profited greatly from their use. But three days ago, I did not understand how I could pray for others without violating their free will, or how God could answer my prayers at the expense of someone else. Now that I've written this chapter, I'm much clearer on the logic of prayer. And much more motivated to pray with passion. I hope you feel the same way.

At the same time, I'm a little embarrassed to have put you through all this logic and reasoning on a subject that is so intuitive and personal. We can spend all our time studying the techniques of fly-fishing but never get our lines wet. The driving simulator I endured during high school driver's ed was a poor substitute for getting in a real car. The best way to learn to pray is to pray.

The greatest Christmas present I ever received as a kid was a Schwinn bicycle. I stared at it all Christmas morning as we slowly unwrapped the rest of our presents. Finally we were done, and I could ride my new bike. The problem was that I didn't have a clue how to do it.

So my father took me outside as I pushed my new bike along. He showed me how the pedals moved the chain and explained the brakes. He demonstrated how the bike would stay up so long as I was balanced over it. He helped me sit on it as he held it up so I could turn the handlebars back and forth. Dad did all he could to explain bicycle engineering to a seven-year-old.

Finally there was nothing else to be learned on the sidewalk. Even though I had more questions than answers and just a little fear at the prospect, I had to actually ride my bike. Dad trotted along beside me, holding me up as I pedaled. Then he released me like a kite into the wind—a kite that crashed after two seconds, that is.

We tried again, and I got a little farther down the road. And even a little farther the next time. Finally I was able to wobble all the way around the cul-de-sac at the end of the street and come back to the house. It was okay that I'd forgotten how the brakes worked—curbs stop bikes very effectively. But I had learned to ride a bike by riding one. And I'll always be glad I left the sidewalk.

For Further Reflection

- Why do you think God wants us to pray continually?
- Why is it important to God that we pray for his glory? How does that kind of praying benefit us?
- Can you think of a time when God did not give you what you asked, but gave you something better in its place? How does this experience relate to the urgency of prayer?
- This chapter suggests that your future prayers can affect past events. What do you think of this idea? How is it relevant to the priority of prayer today?
- Are you waiting for God to answer a prayer today? After reading this chapter, are you more convinced or less convinced that he will do just that?

CONCLUSION

A Man with Two Names

Jacob was the first person recorded in Scripture to wrestle with God. When his match was over, the man named *Deceiver* by his parents would never be the same. Across forty centuries he has been known as Israel, meaning *one who wrestled with God* (Genesis 32:28).

For most of my Christian life, I have been a Jacob. I have tried to convince myself and others that my faith was certain, my questions all answered. It's difficult to trust a dentist with rotten teeth or a pastor who has issues with God. So I've smiled at their questions and answered them with assurance, all the while working hard to sound more confident than I really was. *Deceiver*, my doubts mocked. But I was too busy to take time and wrestle with God for the answers. Or maybe I was afraid of what would happen if I did. I reasoned that a challenge you haven't tried to defeat is better than one you faced and failed.

But there's a ceiling on how closely we can walk with a God we're afraid to understand, and this book is my attempt at being honest with the Lord and with my own soul. I've given myself permission to ask my hardest questions about God and follow the truth wherever it leads. The truth has led to this book and this conclusion: I know much more now than I did when I started. I've settled (at least for myself) some of the most perplexing issues the Christian faith must face. But now that I can claim the name Israel, I know that the match is far from over.

Israel would continue to wrestle with God to the day he died. He still had his estranged brother, Esau, to confront, God to meet at Bethel, his son Joseph to lose and regain. We won't be done with our questions until we stand before the One who is the way, the truth, and the life.

So I'm going to go on wrestling with God. I'm going to ask my hard questions and trust his Word and Spirit for the answers I need. I'm going to believe more than I can understand and trust more than I can prove. I'm going to step into the flooded Jordan before it stops, march around Jericho before it falls, and claim the promised land before it's mine. I'm going to leave my nets so I can fish for men and get out of my boat so I can walk on the water. I'm going to follow my Lord, whether he leads me to a dungeon in Rome or a cave on Patmos. Because wherever I go, he'll be waiting for me.

One day I'll finish wrestling. On that day, when every knee bows and every tongue confesses that Jesus Christ is Lord, he'll invite me to ask my questions and express my doubts. And I'll say with doubting Thomas, "My Lord and my God!" (John 20:28).

I hope you'll join me.

APPENDIX

A Response to Christopher Hitchens and Sam Harris

In the early chapters of this book we listened to atheists Christopher Hitchens and Sam Harris making their case for atheism. Both purport to be spokesmen for a reasoned worldview. Both claim to cite evidence that disproves the Christian faith. Both want us to abandon that faith and approach the world as they do. And while both have largely faded from prominence since this book was first written, their thoughts remain foundational to the way many in our culture understand both God and religion.

Before you do the same, though, you might want to look more closely at their arguments. Consider first some of Hitchens's more remarkable assertions and see if you find him a trustworthy guide to the world of religion.

In *God Is Not Great: How Religion Poisons Everything,* we learn that "Augustine was a self-centered fantasist and an earth-centered ignoramus."[83] Of course, the fact is that the majority of scholars are united in their belief that St. Augustine was one of the greatest intellects in human history. But Hitchens knows better.

Hitchens assures us that "all attempts to reconcile faith with science and reason are consigned to failure."[84] All without exception? Christians who are scientists should definitely take note.

Hitchens describes Mel Gibson's *The Passion of the Christ* as "an exercise in sadomasochistic homoeroticism starring a talentless lead actor who was apparently born in Iceland or Minnesota."[85] I guess Gibson's long list of awards for the movie doesn't count.

Hitchens raises my hackles when he describes C. S. Lewis's reasoning as "so pathetic as to defy description."[86] Lewis took three *firsts* from Oxford University: in Greek and Latin literature, philosophy and ancient history, and English language and literature. (This would be comparable to graduating summa cum laude at Harvard three times.) I'll admit that Lewis is my favorite theologian of the twentieth century, but he is also widely considered the most influential apologist of the modern era. Meanwhile, Hitchens's criticism comes from a man who titled chapter 10 of his diatribe "The Tawdriness of the Miraculous and the Decline of Hell"[87] but failed to discuss hell in the chapter at all.

He is convinced that "the whole racket of American evangelism was just that: a heartless con run by the second-string characters from Chaucer's 'Pardoner's Tale.'"[88] I guess Hitchens must be right, and all the Americans who named Billy Graham the most admired person in the world are wrong.

Hitchens and the Bible

Hitchens has plenty of specific criticisms of God's Word and the Christian faith. I'll respond to a number of them, of varying degrees of significance. Let's begin with the shocking disclosure that "all three monotheisms [Judaism, Christianity, and Islam] . . . praise Abraham for being willing to hear voices and then to take his son Isaac for a long and rather mad and gloomy walk."[89] Of course, the Qur'an teaches that Abraham sacrificed Ishmael, not Isaac—a crucial point in Muslim theology. Hitchens got wrong a fact any first-semester world religions student would know.

We're told that "the New Testament has Saint Paul expressing both fear and contempt for the female."[90] Yet Hitchens includes no citations or evidence to back that up.

Next, Hitchens thinks he can prove in a paragraph that the Bible has no claim on divine inspiration:

> How can it be proven in one paragraph that [the Bible] was written by ignorant men and not by any god? Because man is given "dominion" over all beasts, fowl and fish. But no dinosaurs or plesiosaurs or pterodactyls are specified, because the authors did not know of their existence, let alone of their supposedly special and immediate creation. Nor are any marsupials mentioned, because Australia—the

> next candidate after Mesoamerica for a new "Eden"—was not on any known map. Most important, in Genesis man is not awarded dominion over germs and bacteria because the existence of these necessary yet dangerous fellow creatures was not known or understood. And if it had been known or understood, it would at once have become apparent that these forms of life had "dominion" over us, and would continue to enjoy it uncontested until the priests had been elbowed aside and medical research at last given an opportunity.[91]

I wish that Hitchens had taken at least a freshman-level introductory class in biblical interpretation. There he would have learned that "dominion" means "to be an effective manager," not to be more powerful than all other life-forms. By Hitchens's logic, the creatures in Eden must not have included anything that could harm Adam and Eve.

In *God Is Not Great*, we're informed that "the divine will was made known by direct contact with randomly selected human beings, who were supposedly vouchsafed unalterable laws that could then be passed on to those less favored."[92] But Old Testament laws were only "unalterable" when repeated in the New Testament. For instance, the dietary laws of Leviticus were not unalterable, as the Jerusalem Council made clear (Acts 15). Again, a first-semester biblical studies class would take Hitchens to task on this.

Hitchens uses the King James Version as his biblical reference, expressing shock to discover that John 7:53–8:11

and Mark 16:9–20 were not part of the original ancient Greek manuscripts.[93] Any modern translation of the New Testament makes that clear, and shows that the passages are in no sense foundational to Christian faith, doctrine, or practice.

Hitchens criticizes the Decalogue for naively implying that previous to the giving of the Law, "murder, adultery, theft, and perjury were permissible."[94] Do the current statutes against murder, theft, and perjury imply the same? Did the writers of the Bill of Rights suffer from such ignorance?

We learn from Hitchens that "the Bible may, indeed does, contain a warrant for trafficking in humans, for ethnic cleansing, for slavery, for bride-price, and for indiscriminate massacre, but we are not bound by any of it because it was put together by crude, uncultured human mammals."[95] Hitchens completely misunderstands the difference between descriptive and prescriptive truth in biblical interpretation. To cite his example, the Bible recognizes the existence of slavery and seeks to limit its damage until it can be eradicated forever.

Hitchens compliments H. L. Mencken, who "irrefutably says" that the New Testament is "a helter-skelter accumulation of more or less discordant documents."[96] Of course, Mencken provides no evidence or warrant whatsoever for this conclusion.

We learn that the Gnostic writings "were of the same period and provenance as many of the subsequently canonical and 'authorized' Gospels."[97] An introduction to Gnostic literature would enlighten Hitchens that these books were written generations after the New Testament was completed.

With a single sentence, Hitchens dismisses the apostolic authorship of the New Testament books when he spouts that Jesus's "illiterate living disciples left us no record and in any event could not have been 'Christians,' since they were never to read those later books in which Christians must affirm belief, and in any case had no idea that anyone would ever found a church on their master's announcements."[98] What about the early church's acceptance of this apostolic authorship? Of course, Hitchens offers no suggested evidence or source materials to support his claim. To the casual reader, it would seem that Hitchens's statement is incontrovertible fact without another side in the debate. The fact is that the apostolic authorship of the New Testament is remarkably well documented by early nonbiblical Christian literature.

Hitchens is delighted to point out that "the contradictions and illiteracies of the New Testament have filled up many books by eminent scholars [he never names names], and have never been explained by any Christian authority except in the feeblest terms of 'metaphor' and 'a Christ of faith.'"[99] He is so tragically wrong on the merits. A number of writers have addressed the so-called contradictions of Scripture and shown the remarkable internal consistency of Scripture.[100]

According to Hitchens, the Bible teaches that "things like thrift, innovation, family life, and so forth are a sheer waste of time" in light of the injunction to "take no thought for the morrow."[101] What a shame that he did not consult a commentary or even a good modern translation of the Bible. Jesus meant that we should not worry about the future, not that we should not prepare for it (as he proved in preparing his disciples for his crucifixion).

We're told in no uncertain terms by Hitchens: "It can be stated with certainty, and on their own evidence, that the Gospels are most certainly not literal truth."[102] We're not privileged to know what evidence Hitchens means, but the gospel writer Luke (for one) would certainly be surprised by the claim (Luke 1:1–4).

Hitchens is certain that "those who say 'Christ died for my sins,' when he did not really 'die' at all, are making a statement that is false in its own terms."[103] Doesn't Hitchens understand that Jesus's death paid the price for our sins? The Bible clearly teaches that "while we still were sinners, Christ died for us" (Romans 5:8). While Jesus's resurrection is obviously crucial to our faith, the reality of his death is the reality of the atonement. It's hard for me to understand how Hitchens does not grasp this simple concept.

Hitchens has his own approach to the issue of evil and suffering:

> If one makes the simple assumption, based on absolutely certain knowledge, that we live on a planet that is still cooling, has a molten core, faults and cracks in its crust, and a turbulent weather system, then there is simply no need for any such anxiety [about suffering and the power of God]. Everything is already explained. I fail to see why the religious are so reluctant to admit this: it would free them from all the futile questions about why god permits so much suffering. But apparently this

> annoyance is a small price to pay in order to keep alive the myth of divine intervention.[104]

Why "god permits so much suffering" is precisely the question! Why he permits a world like this or does not intervene when it creates suffering is the issue. And what about moral sin and suffering?

We learn that "if Adam was condemned to death by sinning, his death must have been postponed, since he contrived to raise a large posterity before actually dying."[105] Of course, the Bible says that "the person who sins shall die" (Ezekiel 18:20 NRSVUE), but it does not mean that the person will die in that moment. Physical death sets in, but the process takes time. Otherwise we would all die when we commit our first sin (well before adulthood for most of us), and the human race would cease.

We're assured that "it is only in the reported observations of Jesus that we find any mention of hell and eternal punishment."[106] What about Revelation 20 and the lake of fire?

Finally, Hitchens informs us that "charity and relief work, while they may appeal to tenderhearted believers, are the inheritors of modernism and the Enlightenment. Before that, religion was spread not by example but as an auxiliary to the more old-fashioned methods of holy war and imperialism."[107] Did Hitchens ever read Acts 2 and 4, which clearly record acts of biblical benevolence? Does he really mean to say that the church did no charitable work before the eighteenth century?

Sam Harris and the Christian Faith

Atheist Sam Harris has written as widely as Hitchens on the problems he finds with religion in general and Christianity in particular. While his tone in *Letter to a Christian Nation* is not as vitriolic as Hitchens's acerbic diatribe, it is no less condemning. And no less inaccurate.

For instance, Harris states that Matthew 27:9–10 "claims to fulfill a saying that it attributes to Jeremiah. The saying actually appears in Zechariah 11:12–13."[108] If Harris had consulted any good commentary on the text, he would have learned that Matthew's record of the thirty silver pieces paid to Judas has allusions not only to Zechariah 11 but also to Jeremiah 19:1–13 and Jeremiah 32:6–9. It was standard practice in Matthew's day for an author to refer only to one source or allusion. We see the same treatment in Mark 1:2–3: "As it is written in the prophet Isaiah, 'See, I am sending my messenger ahead of you, who will prepare your way, the voice of one crying out in the wilderness: "Prepare the way of the Lord; make his paths straight."'" Here Mark clearly quotes from both Isaiah 40:3 as well as Malachi 3:1, though he cites only Isaiah by name.

Harris further claims that "the Gospels also contradict one another outright. John tells us that Jesus was crucified the day before the Passover meal was eaten; Mark says it happened the day after. In light of such discrepancies, how is it possible for you to believe that the Bible is perfect in all its parts?"[109]

Apparently Harris bases his claim on John 13:1: "Now before the festival of the Passover, Jesus knew that his hour had come to depart from this world and go to the Father.

Having loved his own who were in the world, he loved them to the end." However, the text does not say that everything that happened subsequent to this verse occurred before the Passover meal, just that "Jesus knew that his hour had come" before the meal began.

In fact, John continues: "The devil had already decided that Judas son of Simon Iscariot would betray Jesus. And *during supper* Jesus, knowing that the Father had given all things into his hands and that he had come from God and was going to God, got up from supper" (John 13:2–4 NRSVUE, emphasis mine). The supper in question was in fact the Passover meal that Harris claims occurred after Jesus's crucifixion. Contradiction resolved.

In one of his most abusive paragraphs, Harris claims:

> God's counsel to parents is straightforward: whenever children get out of line, we should beat them with a rod (Proverbs 13:24, 20:30, and 23:13–14). If they are shameless enough to talk back to us, we should kill them (Leviticus 20:9, Deuteronomy 21:18–21, Mark 7:9–13, and Matthew 15:4–7). We must also stone people to death for heresy, adultery, homosexuality, working on the Sabbath, worshipping graven images, practicing sorcery, and a wide variety of other imaginary crimes.[110]

Proverbs 20:30 has nothing to do with parenting. Exodus 21:15 actually says, "Whoever *strikes* father or mother shall be put to death," (NRSVUE) not whoever "talks back to us."

Harris also misquotes Leviticus 20:9, which speaks of children who "curse" their parents. Mark 7:9–13 and Matthew 15:4–7 quote the commandment but do not apply it. Harris clearly does not understand the hermeneutical principle by which the New Testament interprets the Old Testament. In the formative era of the Hebrew nation, parental respect and family morality were crucial to the survival of the people. These statements are nowhere taught as laws in the New Testament, although the New Testament does retain the principle that children must respect and obey their parents (Ephesians 6:1–3).

Harris misunderstands the biblical statements regarding slavery,[111] citing Leviticus 25:44–46 as proof. In fact, this passage kept the Israelites from enslaving each other. Harris complains that "there is no place in the New Testament where Jesus objects to the practice of slavery."[112] Although it is never specifically mentioned in the New Testament that Jesus objected to slavery, or for that matter racism, genocide, or rape, he did lay the moral foundation upon which later New Testament writers would call for universal equality and justice. Harris then cites Paul's statements that modified slavery and protected slaves (Ephesians 6:5; 1 Timothy 6:1–4), but nowhere mentions Galatians 3:26–29 and its equality for slaves and free. Now comes one of Harris's more outlandish criticisms:

> If a man discovers on his wedding night that his bride is not a virgin, he must stone her to death on her father's doorstep (Deuteronomy 22:13–21). If we are civilized, we will reject this as the vilest lunacy imaginable. Doing so requires that we exercise our own moral

> intuitions. The belief that the Bible is the word of God is of no help to us whatsoever.[113]

A basic course in hermeneutics would help Harris understand that the Deuteronomy test is not required of all believers across all time, that the New Testament interprets the Old, and that this code was required for a nation beginning its spiritual life and cultural existence.

Harris is convinced that all creationists think the universe is six thousand years old. I am a creationist, that is, a person who believes that "God created the heavens and the earth" (Genesis 1:1). But I see no reason whatsoever to affirm a young earth theory. If the universe is 13.8 billion years old (the prevailing consensus), it's fine with me.

Like many critics, Harris misunderstands the purpose of the Scripture with regard to scientific calculation and accuracy:

> In two places, for instance, the Good Book states that the ratio of the circumference of a circle to its diameter is 3:1 (I Kings 7:23–26 and II Chronicles 4:2–5). As an approximation of the constant π, this is not impressive. The decimal expansion of π runs to infinity—3.1415926535. . .—and modern computers now allow us to calculate it to any degree of accuracy we like. But the Egyptians and Babylonians both approximated π to a few decimal places several centuries before the oldest books of the Bible were written. The Bible offers us an approximation that is

> terrible even by the standards of the ancient world. As should come as no surprise, the faithful have found ways of rationalizing this; but those rationalizations cannot conceal the obvious deficiency of the Bible as a source of mathematical insight. It is absolutely true to say that if the Greek mathematician Archimedes had written the relevant passages in I Kings and II Chronicles, the text would bear much greater evidence of the author's "omniscience."[114]

Here's the biblical text in question, referring to a large basin (the sea) located outside the Temple:

> Then he made the molten sea; it was round, ten cubits from brim to brim, and five cubits high. A line of thirty cubits would encircle it completely. Under its brim were gourds all around it, each of ten cubits, surrounding the sea; there were two rows of gourds, cast when it was cast. It stood on twelve oxen, three facing north, three facing west, three facing south, and three facing east; the sea was set on them. The hindquarters of each were toward the inside. Its thickness was a handbreadth; its brim was made like the brim of a cup, like the flower of a lily. (1 Kings 7:23–26 NRSVUE; repeated in 2 Chronicles 4:2–5)

In fact, the Babylonians used 3.125 to approximate π as early as 2000 BC. Archimedes (ca. 250 BC) determined π to be 22/7, or about 3.1418. But of course, calculating the exact circumference of the molten sea used at the Temple was nowhere near the intended purpose of the narrative.

The text simply states that the sea was thirty cubits in circumference, so that "a line of thirty cubits would encircle it completely." Such a distance to the nearest cubit was sufficient for the author's purpose.

Harris is also quite willing to subject his reader to gross exaggeration, such as: "The maintenance of religious dogma *always* comes at the expense of science."[115] As an example, he says that religion claims "if you do not believe the right things about God, you will suffer terribly after death. Such claims are intrinsically in conflict with the claims of science, because they are claims made on terrible evidence."[116] I'm not sure how science can be sure what happens to us after death.

Harris is equally wrong in asserting that "any honest reading of the biblical account of creation suggests that God created all animals and plants *as we now see them*. There is no question that the Bible is wrong about this."[117] Read the first two chapters of Genesis and ask yourself how many animals and plants are described in such precise detail to identify them as the same varieties and species we see today. The answer is exactly none.

A Closing Word

I read Hitchens and Harris in hopes of finding an objective, informed representation of atheism. I was not prepared for the vitriol and inaccuracies that they employed in attacking the Bible and the Christian faith. When critics are this intent on misstating their opponent's views and beliefs, I am left to wonder what insecurities they feel about their own position.

The good news about Christianity is that it is indeed news—a worldview based on historical facts. Hitchens and Harris have not suddenly uncovered evidence that destroys or even damages this faith handed down across twenty centuries. A man who attacks an iron anvil with a stick doesn't damage the anvil. But he'd better get a bigger stick.

RECOMMENDED READING

Barbour, Ian G. *When Science Meets Religion: Enemies, Strangers, or Partners?* HarperCollins, 2000.

Blomberg, Craig L. *The Historical Reliability of the Gospels.* InterVarsity Press, 1987.

Bruce, F. F. *The New Testament Documents: Are They Reliable?* InterVarsity Press, 1977.

Clark, Kelly James. *Return to Reason.* Eerdmans, 1990.

Copan, Paul, and Ronald K. Tacelli, eds. *Jesus's Resurrection: Fact or Figment? A Debate Between William Lane Craig and Gerd Ludemann.* InterVarsity Press, 2000.

Craig, William Lane. *Reasonable Faith: Christian Truth and Apologetics.* Crossway Books, 1994.

Cronin, Vincent. *The View from Planet Earth: Man Looks at the Cosmos.* William Morrow, 1981.

Davis, Stephen, Daniel Kendall, and Gerald O'Collins, eds. *The Resurrection: An Interdisciplinary Symposium on the Resurrection of Jesus.* Oxford University Press, 1997.

Dunn, James D. G. *The Evidence for Jesus.* Westminster Press, 1985.

Dyrness, William. *Christian Apologetics in a World Community.* InterVarsity Press, 1983.

Erickson, Millard J. *Postmodernizing the Faith: Evangelical Responses to the Challenge of Postmodernism.* Baker, 1998.

Fackre, Gabriel J., Ronald H. Nash, and John Sanders. *What About Those Who Have Never Heard? Three Views on the Destiny of the Unevangelized.* Edited by John Sanders. InterVarsity Press, 1995.

France, R. T. *The Evidence for Jesus.* InterVarsity Press, 1986.

Gill, Jerry H. *Faith in Dialogue: A Christian Apologetic.* Word Books, 1985.

Glynn, Patrick. *God: The Evidence: The Reconciliation of Faith and Reason in a Postsecular World.* Forum, 1997.

Goulder, Michael, ed. *Incarnation and Myth: The Debate Continued.* Eerdmans, 1979.

Grenz, Stanley J. *A Primer on Postmodernism.* Eerdmans, 1996.

Habermas, Gary, and Antony Flew. *Did Jesus Rise from the Dead? The Resurrection Debate.* Edited by Terry L. Miethe. Harper & Row, 1987.

Hawking, Stephen. *A Brief History of Time: From the Big Bang to Black Holes.* Bantam Books, 1988.

Herrick, James A. *The Making of the New Spirituality: The Eclipse of the Western Religious Tradition.* InterVarsity Press, 2003.

Hick, John. *Disputed Questions in Theology and the Philosophy of Religion.* Yale University Press, 1993.

Hick, John. *God Has Many Names.* Westminster Press, 1982.

Hick, John, and Brian Hebblethwaite, eds. *Christianity and Other Religions: Selected Readings.* Fortress Press, 1980.

Hick, John, Clark H. Pinnock, Alister E. McGrath, R. Douglas Geivett, and W. Gary Phillips. *Four Views on Salvation in a Pluralistic World.* Zondervan, 1996.

Hock, Dee. *Birth of the Chaordic Age.* Berrett-Koehler, 1999.

Jaki, Stanley L. *The Savior of Science.* Eerdmans, 2000.

Johnson, Phillip E. *Reason in the Balance: The Case Against Naturalism in Science, Law and Education.* InterVarsity Press, 1995.

Kuhn, Thomas S. *The Structure of Scientific Revolutions.* University of Chicago Press, 1996.

Kurzweil, Ray. *The Age of Spiritual Machines: When Computers Exceed Human Intelligence.* Viking, 1999.

Lewis, Gordon R. *Testing Christianity's Truth Claims: Approaches to Christian Apologetics.* Moody Press, 1976.

Mayers, Ronald B. *Both/And: A Balanced Apologetic.* Moody Press, 1984.

McGrath, Alister. *The Science of God.* Eerdmans, 2004.

McGrath, Alister. *The Twilight of Atheism: The Rise and Fall of Disbelief in the Modern World.* Doubleday, 2004.

McGrath, Alister, and Joanna Collicutt McGrath. *The Dawkins Delusion? Atheistic Fundamentalism and the Denial of the Divine.* InterVarsity Press, 2007.

Moreland, J. P., ed. *The Creation Hypothesis: Scientific Evidence for an Intelligent Designer.* InterVarsity Press, 1994.

Moreland, J. P., and Kai Neilson. *Does God Exist? The Great Debate.* Thomas Nelson, 1990.

Nash, Ronald H. *Is Jesus the Only Savior?* Zondervan, 1994.

Phillips, Timothy R., and Dennis L. Okholm, eds. *Christian Apologetics in the Postmodern World.* InterVarsity Press, 1995.

Pinnock, Clark H. *A Wideness in God's Mercy: The Finality of Jesus Christ in a World of Religions.* Zondervan, 1992.

Pinnock, Clark H., ed. *The Grace of God and the Will of Man.* Bethany House Publishers, 1989.

Pinnock, Clark, Richard Rice, John Sanders, William Hasker, and David Basinger. *The Openness of God: A Biblical Challenge to the Traditional Understanding of God.* InterVarsity Press, 1994.

Placher, William C. *Unapologetic Theology: A Christian Voice in a Pluralistic Conversation.* Westminster/John Knox Press, 1989.

Plantinga, Alvin. *Warranted Christian Belief.* Oxford University Press, 2000.

Plantinga, Cornelius, Jr. *Beyond Doubt: Faith-Building Devotions on Questions Christians Ask.* Eerdmans, 2002.

Ramm, Bernard. *The Christian View of Science and Scripture.* Eerdmans, 1954.

Sanders, John. *No Other Name: An Investigation into the Destiny of the Unevangelized.* Eerdmans, 1992.

Sheler, Jeffery L. *Is the Bible True? How Modern Debates and Discoveries Affirm the Essence of the Scriptures.* HarperCollins, 1999.

Sire, James W. *The Universe Next Door: A Basic Worldview Catalog.* 3rd ed. InterVarsity Press, 1997.

Sire, James W. *Why Should Anyone Believe Anything at All?* InterVarsity Press, 1994.

Sobosan, Jeffrey G. *Romancing the Universe: Theology, Science, and Cosmology.* Eerdmans, 1999.

Stackhouse, John G., Jr. *Humble Apologetics: Defending the Faith Today.* Oxford University Press, 2002.

Stannard, Russell, ed. *God for the 21st Century.* Templeton Foundation Press, 2000.

Sweet, Leonard I. *Quantum Spirituality: A Postmodern Apologetic.* Whaleprints, 1991.

Vroom, Hendrik. *No Other Gods: Christian Belief in Dialogue with Buddhism, Hinduism, and Islam.* Translated by Lucy Jansen. Eerdmans, 1996.

ABOUT DR. JIM DENISON

JIM DENISON, PHD, is a cultural theologian and the founder and CEO of Denison Ministries. He speaks biblically into significant cultural issues through *The Daily Article* at DenisonForum.org. He is the author of over 30 books, including *The Coming Tsunami: Why Christians Are Labeled Intolerant, Irrelevant, Oppressive, and Dangerous—and How We Can Turn the Tide*; *Respectfully, I Disagree: How to Be a Civil Person in an Uncivil Time*; and the *Biblical Insight to Tough Questions* series.

He has taught the philosophy of religion and apologetics at several seminaries. Dr. Denison serves as Resident Scholar for Ethics with Baylor Scott & White Health, where he addresses issues such as genetic medicine and reproductive science. He is a senior fellow with Dallas Baptist University's Institute for Global Engagement.

He holds a Doctor of Philosophy and a Master of Divinity degree from Southwestern Baptist Theological Seminary. He also received an honorary Doctor of Divinity degree from Dallas Baptist University. Dr. Denison is the Theologian in Residence for the Baptist General Convention of Texas.

Prior to launching Denison Forum in 2009, he pastored churches in Texas and Georgia. Jim and his wife, Janet, have two married sons and four grandchildren.

ABOUT DENISON MINISTRIES

DENISON MINISTRIES is a nonprofit that equips and disciples followers of Jesus Christ with biblical truth, empowering them to think critically, live faithfully, and serve intentionally to cultivate flourishing communities. The ministry accomplishes that through four distinct brands:

- **Denison Forum (DenisonForum.org)** offers a biblical and redemptive perspective on current events through *The Daily Article* email newsletter and the *Faith & Clarity* podcast, and many other online resources and books.
- **Christian Parenting (ChristianParenting.org)** provides practical and spiritual resources, including an expansive podcast network, to help parents raise children to know and love the Lord.
- **First15 (First15.org)** leads Christians into a transformative personal encounter with God through devotional readings, worship videos, and guided prayers.
- **Foundations (FoundationsWithJanet.org)** offers Bible studies for individual and small-group use.

Learn more at DenisonMinistries.org.

ABOUT DENISON FORUM

DENISON FORUM exists to thoughtfully engage with the issues of our day from a biblical perspective, helping believers discern today's news and culture through the lens of faith. Led by Dr. Jim Denison and a team of contributing writers, we offer trusted insight through *The Daily Article*, a daily email newsletter and podcast, along with articles, podcasts, interviews, books, and other resources. Together, these form a growing ecosystem of Christ-centered content that equips readers to respond to current events not with fear or partisanship, but with clarity, conviction, and hope.

To learn more visit DenisonForum.org.

ALSO FROM DENISON FORUM

The Daily Article email newsletter is news discerned differently every Monday through Friday. Subscribe for free at DenisonForum.org.

Walking in His Commands: A Lenten Journey with Jesus

Love the Lord Your God: A 30-Day Devotional on Christ's Greatest Commandments

Who Am I? What the Bible Says About Identity and Why it Matters

Sacred Sexuality: Reclaiming God's Design

Matthew: A Guide to Genuine Discipleship

Awaken My Heart: A Lent Devotional

Bold Faith

The Path to Purpose

The Fifth Great Awakening and the Future of America

How Does God See America?

What Are My Spiritual Gifts?

Request these books and more at DenisonForum.org/store.

ENDNOTES

Introduction

1. Quoted in Dean Hamer, *The God Gene: How Faith Is Hardwired into Our Genes* (Anchor Books, 2004), 197.
2. Sam Harris, *Letter to a Christian Nation* (Alfred A. Knopf, 2005), 64–65.
3. Harris, *Letter*, 67.

Chapter 1

4. Christopher Hitchens, *God Is Not Great: How Religion Poisons Everything* (Twelve, 2007), 151.
5. Hitchens, *God Is Not Great*, 282.
6. Hitchens, *God Is Not Great*, 12.
7. Hitchens, *God Is Not Great*, 56.
8. Hitchens, *God Is Not Great*, 56.
9. Hitchens, *God Is Not Great*, 60.
10. Harris, *Letter*, 51.
11. Harris, *Letter*, viii.
12. Harris, *Letter*, 57–58.
13. The New Testament list we use today was set forth by Athanasius in AD 367 and approved by church councils meeting at Hippo Regius in 393 and Carthage in 397. But these councils did not choose the books of the New Testament. They simply affirmed what the church had believed for generations.
14. F. F. Bruce, *The New Testament Documents: Are They Reliable?* (Inter-Varsity Press, 1977), 27.
15. Dan Brown, *The Da Vinci Code* (Doubleday, 2003), 231, emphasis his.
16. Brown, *The Da Vinci Code*, 256.
17. For a more in-depth discussion of the evidence for biblical authority, please see my book *The Bible: You Can Believe It—Biblical Authority in the Twenty-First Century* (BaptistWay, 2005).
18. Bruce, *The New Testament Documents*, 19–20.

19. Brown, *The Da Vinci Code*, 245.

20. Brown, *The Da Vinci Code*, 167.

21. Brown, *The Da Vinci Code*, 255.

Chapter 2

22. J. P. Moreland and Kai Nielsen, *Does God Exist? The Great Debate* (Thomas Nelson, 1990), 35.

23. Harris, *Letter*, 51.

24. See for instance, Kai Nielsen, "No! A Defense of Atheism," in *Does God Exist?*, 48–63.

25. Harris, *Letter*, 52.

Chapter 3

26. Hitchens, *God Is Not Great*, 6.

27. Hitchens, *God Is Not Great*, 13, emphasis his.

28. Hitchens, *God Is Not Great*, 52.

29. Harris, *Letter*, 25.

30. Harris, *Letter*, 30.

31. Harris, *Letter*, 30.

32. Harris, *Letter*, 31.

33. Harris, *Letter*, 39.

34. Harris, *Letter*, 40.

35. Harris, *Letter*, 44.

36. Harris, *Letter*, 45.

37. Harris, *Letter*, 54.

38. Hitchens, *God Is Not Great*, 6.

39. Hitchens, *God Is Not Great*, 13.

40. Harris, *Letter*, 44.

41. Harris, *Letter*, 25.

42. Jon Meacham, "The God Debate," *Newsweek*, April 9, 2007, 58.

43. Harris, *Letter*, 90–91.

Chapter 4

44. Mara bar-Serapion, letter, quoted in "Mara bar-Serapion," Early Christian Writings, accessed November 15, 2025, http://www.earlychristianwritings.com/mara.html.

45. Suetonius, *The Lives of the Twelve Caesars*, ed. Joseph Gavorse (Modern Library, 1931), 250.

46. Tacitus, "The Annals," *Great Books of the Western World*, 2nd ed., vol. 14, ed. Mortimer J. Adler (Encyclopedia Britannica, 1990), 168.

47. Pliny, *Letters* 10.96, quoted in R. T. France, *The Evidence for Jesus* (InterVarsity Press, 1986), 42.

48. Flavius Josephus, *Antiquities of the Jews*, trans. William Whiston (Kregel Publications, 1978), 423.

49. Josephus, *Antiquities of the Jews*, 379.

50. "The Didache," *The Early Church Fathers*, ed. E. Glenn Hinson (Broadman Press, 1980), 34.

51. John Keith, trans., *Ante-Nicene Fathers*, vol. 9, ed. Allan Menzies (Buffalo, NY: Christian Literature Publishing Co., 1896), revised and edited for New Advent by Kevin Knight, www.newadvent.org/fathers/1010.htm.

52. "Ignatius to the Smyrnaeans," *The Early Church Fathers*, 151.

53. "The Apologies of Justin," *The Early Church Fathers*, 182–83.

54. "The Apologies of Justin," 179–81.

55. C. S. Lewis, *Mere Christianity* (Macmillan, 1943), 55–56.

56. Gary Habermas and Antony Flew, *Did Jesus Rise from the Dead? The Resurrection Debate* (Harper & Row, 1987), 23.

57. Moreland and Nielsen, *Does God Exist?*, 40.

58. Moreland and Nielsen, *Does God Exist?*, 40.

59. David Hume, *An Enquiry Concerning Human Understanding* (Open Court, 1966), 128–29.

60. Their critics' statement that they were "uneducated and ordinary men" (Acts 4:13 NRSVUE) meant that they had not attended the rabbinic schools (the seminaries of the day), not that they were unintelligent or uneducated.

Chapter 5

61. "The Treatises of Cyprian," *The Ante-Nicene Fathers*, vol. 5, ed. Alexander Roberts and James Donaldson (repr. Eerdmans, 1986), 423.

62. Martin Luther, "Here I Stand," speech, Diet of Worms, Worms, Germany, April 1521.

63. John Calvin, *Calvin: Institutes of the Christian Religion*, ed. McNeill (John T. Westminster, 1960), 69, (1.6.1), https://zondervanacademic.com/blog/john-calvins-institutes-161.

64. John Calvin, *Calvin: Institutes of the Christian Religion*, 1.7.1, https://www.ccel.org/ccel/calvin/institutes.iii.viii.html.

65. From the *Brihadaranyaka Upanishad*, in *Sacred Texts of the World: A Universal Anthology*, ed. Ninian Smart and Richard D. Hecht (Crossroad, 1982), 193.

66. Commentary on the Bhagavad-Gita, in *Sacred Texts*, 203.

Chapter 6

67. The text in English can be found in G. W. Leibniz, *Theodicy: Essays on the Goodness of God, the Freedom of Man, and the Origin of Evil*, trans. E. M. Huggard (Open Court, 1985). The text in chapter 6 is my translation that I did as part of my doctoral work.

68. Boethius, *The Consolation of Philosophy* (Elliot Stock, 1897), 23.

69. Arthur Schopenhauer, *The World as Will and Representation*, trans. E. F. J. Payne, vol. 1 (Dover, 1966), 325, https://ia804500.us.archive.org/19/items/the-world-as-will-and-representation/The-World-as-Will-and-Representation.pdf.

70. Irenaeus saw man at his creation as "infantile" and theorized that "It was necessary that man should in the first instance be created; and having been created, should receive growth; and having received growth, should be strengthened; and having been strengthened, should abound; and having abounded, should recover [from the disease of sin]; and having recovered, should be glorified; and being glorified, should see his Lord." Quoted from "Against Heresies," *The Ante-Nicene Fathers*, vol. 1, ed. Alexander Roberts and James Donaldson (Eerdmans, 1989), 521–522.

71. John Hick describes the Irenaean view of the fall: "Irenaeus pictures Adam and Eve in the Garden of Eden as children; and their sin is accordingly not presented as a damnable revolt, but rather as calling forth

God's compassion on account of their weakness and vulnerability." John Hick, *Evil and the God of Love,* (Harper & Row, 1978), 212.

Chapter 7

72. The stabbing victim Christopher McCarthy did survive. See https://web.archive.org/web/20100102134627/http://houstonist.com/2006/06/21/houston_stabbin.php.

73. William Revell Moody, *The Life of Dwight L. Moody* (Fleming H. Revell, 1900), 552.

Chapter 9

74. David K. Barrett, George T. Kurian, and Todd M. Johnson, *World Christian Encyclopedia*, vol. 1, 2nd ed. (Oxford University Press, 2001), 4.

75. John Sanders, *No Other Name: An Investigation into the Destiny of the Unevangelized* (Eerdmans, 1992), 15–16; also Barrett et al., *World Christian Encyclopedia.*

76. Conrad Hackett et al., *How the Global Religious Landscape Changed from 2010 to 2020* (Pew Research Center, 2025), https://www.pewresearch.org/religion/2025/06/09/how-the-global-religious-landscape-changed-from-2010-to-2020/.

77. "Dreams and Visions of Isa al Masih," www.IsaAlMasih.net.

78. C. S. Lewis, *The Problem of Pain* (Macmillan, 1977), 127–28.

79. Calvin Miller, *The Singer* (InterVarsity Press, 1975), 129.

80. John Milton, *Paradise Lost*, vol. 1, line 262, in *Complete Poems and Major Prose*, ed. Merritt Y. Hughes (Odyssey, 1959), 218.

Chapter 11

81. All quotations from the Qur'an are from Abdullah Yusuf Ali, *The Qur'an: Text, Translation and Commentary*, vol. 2 (Tahrike Tarsile Qur'an, 2005), 136.

82. Ali, *The Qur'an*, vol. 4, 171.

Appendix

83. Hitchens, *God Is Not Great*, 64.

84. Hitchens, *God Is Not Great*, 64–65.

85. Hitchens, *God Is Not Great*, 111.

86. Hitchens, *God Is Not Great*, 120.

87. Hitchens, *God Is Not Great*, 139.

88. Hitchens, *God Is Not Great*, 160.

89. Hitchens, *God Is Not Great*, 53.

90. Hitchens, *God Is Not Great*, 54.

91. Hitchens, *God Is Not Great*, 90, emphasis in the original.

92. Hitchens, *God Is Not Great*, 97.

93. Hitchens, *God Is Not Great*, 120–22, 142.

94. Hitchens, *God Is Not Great*, 99.

95. Hitchens, *God Is Not Great*, 102.

96. Hitchens, *God Is Not Great*, 110.

97. Hitchens, *God Is Not Great*, 112.

98. Hitchens, *God Is Not Great*, 114.

99. Hitchens, *God Is Not Great*, 115.

100. See *The Bible: You Can Trust It* (BaptistWay Press, 2005), 33–45.

101. Hitchens, *God Is Not Great*, 118.

102. Hitchens, *God Is Not Great*, 120.

103. Hitchens, *God Is Not Great*, 143.

104. Hitchens, *God Is Not Great*, 149.

105. Hitchens, *God Is Not Great*, 156.

106. Hitchens, *God Is Not Great*, 175.

107. Hitchens, *God Is Not Great*, 192.

108. Harris, *Letter*, 58.

109. Harris, *Letter*, 58–59.

110. Harris, *Letter*, 8.

111. Harris, *Letter*, 14–19.

112. Harris, *Letter*, 16.

113. Harris, *Letter*, 50.

114. Harris, *Letter*, 60–61.

115. Harris, *Letter*, 63, emphasis his.

116. Harris, *Letter*, 64.

117. Harris, *Letter*, 71, emphasis mine.